SINGULAR/PLURAL

A noun may either be **singular** (one thing) or **plural** (more than one) in form. To form the plural of a noun, you usually add *s* or *es* to the end of the singular form:

rat/rats	peach/peaches
car/cars	potato/potatoes
echo/echoes	exercise/exercises

For some nouns, you will need to change letters when forming the plural:

wolf/wolves	elf/elves
baby/babies	mystery/mysteries
goose/geese	woman/women

The singular and plural forms of a few nouns are the same:

sheep　fish　deer　salmon

HINTS

A. Certain clues will help you identify nouns. For instance, words that come right before the verb (action word) in a sentence are often nouns:

1. The tall <u>girl</u> won the race.
2. <u>Jack</u> read the book three times.
3. My <u>grandma</u> wishes it never rained.

B. Also , the three articles—*a*, *an*, and *the*—signal that a noun will follow:

1. The man in the red coat is a <u>musician</u>.
2. The hawk killed the <u>mouse</u>.
3. Bill eats an <u>apple</u> every morning.

NOUN EXERCISES

A. *Directions:* Underline the nouns in the following sentences.
EXAMPLE: <u>Tina</u> loves <u>gum</u> and <u>ice cream</u>.

LIFE OF THE HOBO

1. <u>Hoboes</u> traveled from <u>place</u> to <u>place</u> and worked in temporary <u>jobs</u>.
2. <u>Hoboes</u> were sometimes called *migratory* <u>workers</u>.
3. In <u>1900</u> many <u>hoboes</u> traveled around the <u>United</u> <u>States</u> on the <u>railroads</u>.
4. These <u>men</u> did not buy <u>tickets</u> but rode in empty <u>boxcars</u> on <u>freight</u> <u>trains</u>.
5. <u>Hundreds</u> of <u>hoboes</u> were killed or hurt on these dangerous <u>rides</u>.
6. <u>Hoboes</u> often spent the <u>night</u> in <u>camps</u> called "jungles."
7. In the <u>winter</u> many <u>hoboes</u> flocked to <u>cities</u> to seek <u>shelter</u>.
8. <u>Hoboes</u> often composed <u>songs</u> and <u>poems</u> about their <u>journeys</u>.
9. Some migratory <u>workers</u> even published their <u>thoughts</u> and <u>opin-ions</u> in a <u>magazine</u> called <u>Hobo</u> <u>News</u>.
10. The <u>life</u> of a <u>hobo</u> could sometimes be sad and lonely.

B. *Directions:* Some words can be used in more than one way. Underline the words below that could be used as nouns.
EXAMPLE: <u>fear</u>　　　though　　　not

to	<u>London</u>	<u>Queen Elizabeth</u>
<u>apple</u>	<u>intelligence</u>	slowly
and	<u>appear</u>	<u>clam</u>
<u>love</u>	<u>orange</u>	<u>red</u>
<u>skunk</u>	into	<u>fish</u>
ugly	<u>song</u>	<u>courage</u>
<u>hope</u>	never	seem
<u>Raymond</u>	<u>mile</u>	<u>river</u>
from	but	<u>frost</u>
<u>idea</u>	<u>month</u>	borrow

C. *Directions*: Insert nouns in the blanks in the following sentences.
EXAMPLE: The ___*clams*___ are delicious.

1. What kind of _____ does _____ like best?
2. The _____ is going to _____ for a _____.
3. The _____ in the _____ is creating a _____.
4. _____ believes that _____ is the most important quality a person can have.
5. Some _____ don't eat _____ in the _____.
6. A small _____ sat quietly by the edge of the _____.
7. The _____ took us most of the _____ to complete.
8. Please bring me a _____ from the _____.
9. I saw _____ and _____ from the _____.
10. _____ joined the _____ last _____.

Answers will vary.

D. *Directions:* Write five sentences of your own and then underline the nouns.

EXAMPLE: <u>Sal</u> ate the <u>plum</u>.

1. _____
2. _____
3. _____
4. _____
5. _____

Answers will vary.

Now read the following sentences and fill in the blanks with the appropriate pronoun:

1. Alice bought a murder mystery. __**It**__ was scary.
2. The teacher is here, Ramon. **You or We** had better be quiet.
3. My parents' oldest child is a boy. He is __**my**__ brother.
4. Ms. Casey won the election. __**She**__ celebrated with friends.
5. My guests arrived early. I gave __**them**__ something to eat.
6. The people next door never lock their back door. A burglar got into __**their**__ house and stole __**their**__ camera.

HINT If you have trouble with any of the sentences above, look at the following chart for help.

SINGULAR

	Subjects	Objects	Possessives
1st person	I	me	my, mine
2nd person	you	you	your, yours
3rd person	he, she, it	him, her, it	his, her, hers, its

PLURAL

	Subjects	Objects	Possessives
1st person	we	us	our, ours
2nd person	you	you	your, yours
3rd person	they	them	their, theirs

PRONOUN EXERCISES

A. *Directions:* Circle the pronouns in the following sentences. Underline the nouns.

EXAMPLE: (He) stole my <u>cookie</u> and ate (it.)

1. Aunt <u>Emily</u> bought (her) a <u>book</u> for <u>Christmas</u>.
2. (They) packed (their) <u>bags</u> and left <u>town</u> quickly.
3. Do (you) think (you) could find (his) <u>name</u> in the <u>phone book</u>?
4. Please save (us) from (her) ferocious <u>hamsters</u>!
5. (I) think (she) likes (me) better than (your) <u>brother</u>.
6. (She) hoped that (she) would see (them) on the <u>way</u> to the <u>park</u>.
7. <u>Sue</u> saw (him) cheating when (she) raised (her) <u>head</u>.
8. (We) did not want to hurt (its) <u>wings</u>.
9. (Those) funny-looking <u>slippers</u> (you) saw are (mine.)
10. How did (he) know (their) <u>friends</u> would not get there on <u>time</u>?

B. *Directions:* In the spaces at the end of each sentence, write the pronouns you would use to replace the italicized nouns.

EXAMPLE: *Ralph* gave the *dog* a bone. ___He___ ___it___

1. *Gillian* bought *Trevor* a pet gorilla. **She** **him**
2. The *hikers* stopped to watch an *eagle* catch a mouse. **They** **it**
3. *Mrs. Rodriguez* confiscated *Billy's* hat during the concert. **She** **his**
4. The *girls* did not like the *novel's* ending. **They** **its**
5. The *family's* house disappeared when the *witch* cast a spell. **Their** **she**
6. The *lion* watched the *gazelles* with great interest. **It** **them**
7. The *rabbit* grabbed the *hunter's* gun and ran away. **It** **his or her**
8. The *audience* applauded when the *movie* ended. **They** **it**
9. Joe borrowed the *car* from the *Parkers'* garage. **it** **their**
10. *Mr. McGiver* baked the *girl* a carrot cake. **He** **her**

Although it is the correct answer for audience, most students will respond with they.

C. *Directions:* Circle the pronouns in the list below that show possession.

EXAMPLE: (her) I us

(our) you (his)
he (mine) me
(your) (their) she
(hers) it (its)
we they (my)

D. *Directions:* Rewrite the following sentences, replacing the italicized pronouns with nouns.

EXAMPLE: *He* wrote *her* a letter.
　　　　Biff wrote Minnie a letter.

1. *He* wished that *her* father were a nicer person.

_____

2. *She* watched *them* jump out of the water.

_____

Answers will vary.

3. VERBS

Read the following sentence and circle the word that tells what Sarah did:

　　Sarah hit the ball through the window.

If you circled *hit*, you're right. Now read the following sentence and circle the word that tells you something about Mr. Belinsky's feeling of sadness:

　　Mr. Belinsky seemed sad.

If you circled *seemed*, you're right again. The word *seemed* tells you something **about** Mr. Belinsky's sadness. He may or may not have actually been sad. What you know for sure is that he **seemed**—or appeared to be—sad.

> **Definition**
> The words *hit* and *seemed* in the above sentences are **verbs**. A **verb** is a word that expresses an action (*run, hurl, swim, fly, sing*) or a state of being (*is, appear, seem, be*). The verb is sometimes called the **predicate**. It either tells you what a noun is doing or provides you with information about the state or condition of that noun. Most verbs are **action verbs**. The much smaller group of verbs that express a state of being are called **linking verbs**. You will be learning more about linking verbs later in this series.

Now circle the verbs in the following sentences:

1. Brian (drove) the car into a ditch.
2. Sharon (is) an excellent engineer.
3. The bubbles (floated) down to the ground.
4. That shaggy dog (looks) happy.

Depending on how they are used, verbs make statements (Sally *walked* to the store.), ask questions (Are you *going* to the concert?), or give commands. (*Give* me that kangaroo!) Read the following sentences and write *statement*, *question*, or *command* in the space provided, depending on what the verb is doing:

1. May I have a drink of water? **question**
2. Throw me that towel. **command**
3. Janice won the marathon. **statement**

HELPING VERBS

Sometimes a verb is preceded by an **auxiliary** or **helping verb**. (Sandy **might** go to the beach.) These helping verbs help the main verb explain in more detail what a noun is doing. For instance, the helping verb *might* in the above sentence tells you that Sandy **may** go to the beach, not that she will definitely go. The verb and its helping verbs together are called **verb phrases**. Circle the verb phrases in the following sentences:

1. I (will fly) to Costa Rica tomorrow.
2. Bob (had read) the book before.
3. Shirley (has been living) in France.
4. Mr. Graham (may have been mistaken.)

As you see, a verb may have one, two, or even three helping verbs. Some of the most common of these helping verbs are: *has, have, had, is, be, been, do, does, did, may, might, will, shall, would,* and *must.*

TENSE

Read the following sentences and write **present**, **past**, or **future** in the spaces provided, depending on when the action took place:

1. Alice will fly the plane next Wednesday. **future**

2. Bill saw the buffalo last summer. **past**

3. Now the fly buzzes on the windowsill. **present**

4. Ramon caught the mouse. **past**

5. Mr. McGovern will travel around China this summer.
   future

6. The car speeds around the corner. **present**

The **tense** of a verb tells you when the action or state of being took place. The three most important tenses are the **present** (It's happening right now: She walks.), the **past** (It already happened: She walked.), and the **future** (It's going to happen—it hasn't happened yet: She will walk.)

The present tense usually ends with *s*. To form the future tense, you use the helping verbs *will* or *shall* with a main verb. To form the past tense, you generally add the letters −*ed*, −*d*, or −*t* to a verb.

Verbs that form the past tense in a different way are **irregular verbs**. To form the past tense of an irregular verb, you must either change a

VERB EXERCISES

A. *Directions:* Underline the verbs in the following sentences twice. Underline the nouns once. Then circle all the pronouns.
   EXAMPLE: (She) wrote to the poet.

A GREAT POET

1. John Keats lived most of (his) life in England.
2. (He) was born in 1795.
3. Keats had two brothers and a sister.
4. (He) studied medicine in school but then became a poet.
5. Keats once went on a walking tour of northern England and Scotland.
6. (He) met William Wordsworth, a famous poet, on several occasions.
7. Keats devoted many hours to (his) poems and rewrote (them) many times.
8. Keats died of tuberculosis when (he) was twenty-five.
9. If (he) had lived, Keats would have written many more poems.
10. Today, Keats is considered one of the greatest English poets.

B. *Directions:* Insert verbs in the blanks in the following sentences.
   EXAMPLE: Gary _____*lifted*_____ the bag from the floor.

1. Sam _____ his dog a bowl of water.

2. _____ Courtney ever _____ again?

3. The farmer _____ to town and _____ her cattle.

4. I _____ _____ to the movies on Thursday.

5. Ramon _____ and _____ all the way home.

6. The president _____ not _____ a decision until he _____ all the facts.

7. What _____ you _____ for your birthday?

8. _____ me the article that you _____ in the magazine.

9. The tornado _____ the town in a few minutes.

10. Lester _____ _____ _____ his father if the concert _____ _____ .

Answers will vary.

C. *Directions:* Underline twice the words that could be used as verbs.

EXAMPLE: <u>scream</u>   now   deep

smack	kiss	elephant
dance	topple	weave
play	yet	stream
gracefully	look	roar
spin	again	sound
rapid	hurt	think
laugh	smell	quickly
boast	feel	sew
ring	wiggle	against
taste	alone	are

D. *Directions:* Using the verb tenses that are indicated, write ten sentences of your own. Then underline the verbs twice.

EXAMPLE: future   I <u>will</u> <u>go</u> to Paris in May.

1. past _____
2. present _____
3. future _____
4. past _____
5. past _____
6. future _____
7. present _____
8. present _____
9. past _____
10. future _____

Answers will vary.

4. SUBJECTS

Read the following sentences and then answer the questions in the spaces provided:

1. Jane rode her horse every week.
   Who rode the horse? **Jane**
2. The enormous alligator ate Chicago.
   What ate Chicago? **alligator**
3. The Starskys flew to Rome yesterday.
   Who flew to Rome? **Starskys**

What do the three words you wrote in the spaces have in common? If you think about the way these words are used in the above sentences, you'll see that all three are *doing* the action of the verbs.

Definition
The **subject** of a sentence is the noun or pronoun that is doing the action of the verb. To put it another way, the subject is the noun or pronoun that is being talked about in a sentence.

In the above sentences, for instance, the words *Jane, alligator,* and *Starskys* are doing the action of the verbs *rode, ate,* and *flew.* The subject is considered to be one of the **functions** of the noun or pronoun.

FINDING THE SUBJECT

Now look at the following sentences and underline the subjects:

1. The <u>cat</u> in the large dead tree chases birds.
2. The <u>beginning</u> of that book bored me.
3. The <u>top</u> of the building is gold.

As you can see, subjects can often be separated from verbs by several other words. If you're not sure what the subject is, just ask yourself the question, "Who or what is doing the action of the verb?"

SUBJECT EXERCISES

A. *Directions:* Write the subject of each sentence in the space at the end.
EXAMPLE: The cat ate the mouse. _____*cat*_____

1917: A REMARKABLE YEAR

1. Many important events occurred in 1917. **events**

2. The first Russian Revolution ended the rule of the tsars in February. **Russian Revolution**

3. President Woodrow Wilson began his second term of office the following month. **President Woodrow Wilson**

4. The United States entered World War I that spring. **United States**

5. T. S. Eliot's poem, "The Love Song of J. Alfred Prufrock," stunned the literary world that year. **"The Love Song of J. Alfred Prufrock"**

6. Many other brilliant young poets died on the battlefields in France. **poets**

7. John F. Kennedy was born in his family's house in Brookline, Massachusetts. **John F. Kennedy**

8. Puerto Ricans were granted United States citizenship. **Puerto Ricans**

9. In October, Lenin led a second revolution in Russia. **Lenin**

10. There are many reasons to spend time reading about that year in history books. **reasons**

B. *Directions:* Insert subjects in the blanks in the following sentences.
EXAMPLE: _____*Arnie*_____ raced Jan to the corner.

1. _____ flew to Moscow on a peace mission.

2. _____ reached out calmly and yanked me into the boat.

3. _____ followed Sally home at the end of the day.

4. _____ is the title of a famous book.

5. _____ rattled the windows at the height of the storm.

6. _____ made me jump in surprise.

7. _____ knew that I was coming to town on Thursday.

8. Did _____ write a terrifying book about vampires?

Answers will vary.

9. _____ sang a song until the baby fell asleep.

10. _____ tasted even worse than usual.

C. *Directions:* Use each of the following words as the subject of a sentence.
EXAMPLE: rat *The rat slithered down the hole.*

1. dentist _____

2. calendar _____

3. sunset _____

4. Argentina _____

5. honesty _____

6. photograph _____

7. president _____

8. computer _____

9. Alexis _____

10. alligator _____

Answers will vary.

D. *Directions:* Write five sentences that begin with *there.* Then write the subject at the end of each sentence.
EXAMPLE: There goes the train. *train*

1. _____

2. _____

3. _____

4. _____

5. _____

Answers will vary.

the names of cities, states, and countries:

Minneapolis   Montana   Australia

the names of deities, religions, and religious organizations:

Jehovah   Hinduism   National Council of Churches

the names of political parties, governing bodies, and governmental departments:

Republican party   Provisional Government
U.S. Justice Department

the names of races, peoples, and languages:

Hispanic   Chinese   Italian

TITLES AND LETTERS

Titles must always be capitalized. This rule applies to books (*Pride and Prejudice*), poems ("The Road Not Taken"), plays (*Romeo and Juliet*), articles ("Travels through Georgia"), stories ("To Build a Fire"), magazines (*The New Yorker*), newspapers (*Washington Post*), essays ("Shooting an Elephant"), movies (*Star Wars*), songs ("Let It Be"), works of art (*Mona Lisa*), and television programs (*I Love Lucy*). In titles, capitalize the first and last words and all other words except prepositions, conjunctions, and articles (*a, an, the*): (*Diary of a Madman and Other Stories*).

Finally, when you are writing a letter, capitalize the first word and all nouns in the salutation or greeting. On the other hand, only capitalize the first word in the closing:

Dear President Lincoln: Yours truly,
Dear Tim and Cindy,   Best wishes,

CAPITALIZATION EXERCISES

A. *Directions:* In the following sentences, circle the letters that should be capitalized.

EXAMPLE: (m)s. (g)omez said that (m)t. (w)ashington is located in (n)ew (h)ampshire.

1. (m)y uncle (j)ack lives on (e)lm (s)treet in (d)enver.
2. (t)he (e)mpire (s)tate (b)uilding was once the tallest building in (n)ew (y)ork.
3. (t)he (b)oston (r)ed (s)ox play baseball in (f)enway (p)ark.

4. (s)wallows and (a)mazons is (b)ill's favorite book.
5. (n)adine's family usually goes to (m)aine in (m)ay or (s)eptember.
6. (t)he (b)eatles had a hit song called "(h)elp."
7. (w)inston (c)hurchill was prime minister of (e)ngland during (w)orld (w)ar II.
8. (d)r. (c)havez grew up in (m)anagua, (n)icaragua.
9. "(m)y (p)apa's (w)altz" is a poem by (t)heodore (r)oethke.
10. (h)ilary paddled the canoe along the (m)ississippi (r)iver from (m)inneapolis to (n)ew (o)rleans.

B. *Directions:* Rewrite each word or group of words, properly capitalized, in the space to the right. If the word or group of words is already capitalized properly, just write *C* in the space.

EXAMPLE: los angeles ___Los Angeles___

1. mister billingsgate ___Mister Billingsgate___
2. *The Name Of The Rose* ___The Name of the Rose___
3. Orthodontist ___orthodontist___
4. mt. mckinley ___Mt. McKinley___
5. *New York Times* ___C___
6. prime minister Thatcher ___Prime Minister Thatcher___
7. Smallpox ___smallpox___
8. *The Sword in the Stone* ___C___
9. Salmon ___salmon___
10. lake superior ___Lake Superior___
11. Romeo and Juliet ___C___
12. easter Sunday ___Easter Sunday___
13. Chicago cubs ___Chicago Cubs___
14. the wind in the willows ___The Wind in the Willows___
15. secretary of State ___secretary of state___

C. *Directions:* In the space to the right of each common noun, write a proper noun that is an example of that common noun. Be sure to capitalize the proper noun correctly.

EXAMPLE: pirate ___Long John Silver___

1. country _____
2. novel _____
3. river _____

Answers will vary.

1. That restaurant is always crowded on weekends **.**
2. What kind of money do they use in Nepal **?**
3. John Wilkes Booth shot Abraham Lincoln at the Ford Theater **.**
4. Watch out for the train **!**
5. Do you think there is any reason to shout **?**
6. An American writer named Ambrose Bierce disappeared in 1914 **.**
7. Ralph, catch the baby **!**
8. Reykjavik is the capital of Iceland **.**
9. Would you consider going to the dance with Josie **?**
10. I can't stop the car **!**

B. *Directions:* If a sentence is punctuated correctly, write **C** in the space at the end of the sentence. If the end punctuation is incorrect, circle it and write the correct punctuation in the space.
EXAMPLE: Did Jane drive the car to the movies⊙ __?__

1. Mao Zedong led a revolution in China in 1949⊙ **.**
2. What would you like to do with your life⊙ __?__
3. Walter spent the summer in Mexico City. __C__
4. I can't stand it anymore⊙ __!__
5. Did Mr. Pringle believe your story about losing your homework? __C__
6. Pip is the main character of the novel *Great Expectations*⊙ **.**
7. Get out of my way! __C__
8. In 1860, millions of buffalo roamed the American prairies⊙ **.**
9. How did Harold lose the goldfish⊙ __?__
10. St. Patrick is the patron saint of Ireland⊙ **.**

C. *Directions:* Write two statements, two questions, and two exclamations. Punctuate each of these sentences with the proper end punctuation.
EXAMPLE: You're stepping on my hand!

1. _____
2. _____
3. _____
4. _____
5. _____
6. _____

Answers will vary.

Emily's opinion of William. Sentences 1 and 2 would also be confusing without commas:

1. After seeing his uncle, Bill bought a paper.
2. Above, the jet roared through the sky.

When you try reading these sentences without commas, you'll see that it is possible to misread them.

DATES, ADDRESSES, AND GEOGRAPHICAL NAMES

Use commas to separate items in dates, addresses, and geographical names:

1. Tuesday, June 29, 1901
2. 6 Duck Street, Grinnell, Iowa
3. Paris, France

LETTERS

Use commas after the salutation of a friendly or informal letter (as opposed to a business letter) and after the closing of any letter:

Dear Aunt May,	Yours truly,
Dear Dad,	Sincerely,

There are a number of other situations in which it is necessary to use commas. You will learn about these situations as you study new concepts later in these books.

COMMA EXERCISES

A. *Directions:* Insert commas where they are needed in the following sentences.
EXAMPLE: By the way, Shirley, how's your parakeet?

1. Gabriela wanted bacon, lettuce, and tomato on her sandwiches.
2. No, I do not want to go to the lecture on dinosaurs.
3. Is that you, Makiba?
4. When she saw her aunt, Martha began to laugh.
5. The spy gave Herman a cold, murderous look.
6. Does Mr. Kaplinsky live in Kansas City, Kansas or Kansas City, Missouri?
7. John Kennedy was assassinated on November 22, 1963.
8. Above, the eagle flew gracefully through the air.
9. The bright young man sat down, ordered his breakfast, and ate it.

10. Oh, why won't you ever listen to me, Thelma?
11. To Betty, Henry looked like a clown.
12. Robert loved to read books by Gogol, Turgenev, Tolstoy, and Chekhov.
13. His smooth, graceful walk revealed that he was a dancer.
14. Ever since, Sam has been scared of angry muskrats.
15. Yes, Rosie, I intend to visit Rome, Italy.

B. *Directions:* Insert commas where they are needed in the following sentences. If a sentence is correct, write the letter **C** in the space at the end.
EXAMPLE: Please bring me a drink, Tim. _C_

1. Well, I don't see why they moved to Houston, Texas. ____
2. Nigel's favorite colors were black, gray, and white. ____
3. Roy, could you help me mow the lawn on Friday, June 10? ____
4. The cool, green water lapped around Matilda's feet. _C_
5. Yes, I think I will go swimming on Mondays, Wednesdays, and Saturdays. ____
6. Now will you roll the dice and move, Billy? _C_
7. Leroy lived at 6 Oakhurst Drive, Springfield, Ohio. ____
8. Running, reading, and fishing were Anne's favorite activities. _C_
9. No, Elvida, you can't put marshmallows in the soup. ____
10. According to his uncle, Harry was a mean, unfriendly boy. ____

C. *Directions:* In the following sentences, circle the commas that are not necessary and insert commas where they are needed.
EXAMPLE: Jane⊘ lived in an old, shabby house.

1. Penelope collects butterflies, coins, bumper stickers, and⊘ stamps.
2. The athletic⊘ senior girls live in Spokane, Washington.
3. Next to her⊘ cousin Jake, June saw an enormous turtle.
4. Well, Phillip, I guess⊘ reading, writing, and math are not your strong points.
5. Woody Guthrie⊘ grew up in Okemah, Oklahoma.
6. Donald saw a group of large, hungry⊘ crocodiles slip into the river.
7. He arrived⊘ in Flatfoot, North Dakota on May 12, 1972.
8. No, I don't believe a word⊘ you are saying, Alice.
9. Gum drops, chocolate, and boiled⊘ sweets are all examples of candy.
10. When⊘ did you become a lawyer, Arturo?

D. *Directions:* Make up sentences that illustrate each of the following situations.
EXAMPLE: commas in dates   *I was born on August 4, 1923.*

1. commas in series _____
   _____

2. commas between adjectives _____
   _____

3. commas to prevent misunderstandings _____
   _____

4. commas after opening words _____
   _____

5. commas in direct address _____
   _____

6. commas in addresses _____
   _____

Answers will vary.

TURNING FRAGMENTS INTO SENTENCES

Now look back at the three sentence fragments at the beginning of this lesson. Add whatever words are necessary to turn these fragments into complete sentences. Then write your sentences in the following spaces:

1. _____
2. _____
3. _____

Answers will vary.

SENTENCE FRAGMENT EXERCISES

A. *Directions:* In the space following each group of words, write *F* if it is a fragment and *S* if it is a sentence.
EXAMPLE: Sam didn't know what. _F_

1. At the beginning of the game on Tuesday. **F**
2. When Mitzi arrived home from the movie. **F**
3. I bought a cat yesterday. **S**
4. With a gleam in her eye and a toss of her head. **F**
5. Ed cried. **S**
6. Why must you always on Thursday? **F**
7. If I had a model train set. **F**
8. Before Bea had a chance to call her name. **F**
9. I suppose I haven't expressed myself clearly. **S**
10. Skimming above the surface of the water a beautiful fish. **F**

B. *Directions:* Rewrite the following fragments so that they are sentences. Be sure to use every word of the fragment in your sentence.
EXAMPLE: If you eat that toadstool.
   If you eat that toadstool, you might die.

1. Whenever I see a grizzly bear.

   _____

2. My favorite rock performer in the world.

   _____

3. In a dusty corner at the back of the attic.

   _____

4. Running through the woods on a cold winter morning.

   _____

Answers will vary.

5. Although Janice had never been to Norway before.

   _____

6. Because I was late for my first class.

   _____

7. Hoping that the bus hadn't left without her.

   _____

8. While we were setting up your tent in the woods.

   _____

9. In the event of a flood or tornado.

   _____

10. Before you read that book about South Africa.

   _____

Answers will vary.

C. *Directions:* Read the following sentence fragments. In the space at the end of each fragment, write *yes* if the fragment contains a subject and verb and *no* if the fragment does not contain a subject and verb.
EXAMPLE: When I saw the fox. _yes_

1. At the end of a long day in the mountains. **no**
2. Even if you do catch the frog. **yes**
3. Since you insist on choosing the turkey. **yes**
4. Above the beautiful, swift river. **no**
5. On top of the bowl of cornflakes. **no**
6. Swimming in the slimy river. **no**
7. Through the dark tunnel out into the sunlight. **no**
8. Because you do not like the mail carrier. **yes**
9. When Carl feeds the peacock. **yes**
10. In the quietest part of the recital. **no**

RUN-ON SENTENCE EXERCISES

A. *Directions:* In the space following each group of words, write *R* if it is a run-on sentence and *S* if it is a sentence.
EXAMPLE: Eric ran to town he missed the bus. _R_

1. Socrates was a famous Greek philosopher. _S_
2. Dan met Sue on the bus then they went to the beach. _R_
3. The bear chased Stephanie, she climbed a tree just in time. _R_
4. We have seen the movie before, we'd like to go again. _R_
5. I don't believe in eating pretzels with a fork. _S_
6. Mr. Rochester hired Jane Eyre to be a governess she fell in love with him. _R_
7. Dark had fallen, it was a stormy night. _R_
8. When I go to a play, I like to get there early. _S_
9. I do not believe in ghosts, they don't really exist. _R_
10. Go dig some clams at the beach bring them back here for dinner. _R_

B. *Directions:* Turn the following run-ons into sentences by putting capital letters where sentences should begin and end punctuation where they should end.
EXAMPLE: Helen bought a house; she loved it.

1. My house wasn't the same anymore. It even smelled different.
2. We went to the fair every day. You could go on three rides for a dollar.
3. Climbing the mountain was hard. I would not do it again.
4. Sailing is her favorite sport. Each weekend she goes to the lake.
5. The magazine finally arrived. Now I can read my article.
6. The hurricane destroyed the house. Everyone inside it was saved.
7. You'd have to see it yourself. I can't describe it in words.
8. The writer finished his book. He began another one right away.
9. Most people buy pumpkins in the fall. They carve them for Halloween.
10. The end of the spy story was exciting. It kept me on the edge of my seat.

C. *Directions:* In the space after each group of words, write *R* if it is a run-on, *F* if it is a fragment, and *S* if it is a sentence.
EXAMPLE: In the dark woods. _F_

1. Riding out the storm on a cold, wild night. _F_
2. After the party, Julie drove home with Miriam. _S_
3. Daryl spent two weeks in the Soviet Union she thought it was a fascinating place. _R_
4. Franklin Roosevelt won reelection in 1940, a year before the United States entered World War II. _S_
5. I think I'll visit Sally maybe she'll want to take a walk. _R_
6. Even though I had never seen such a beautiful sunset on a winter day. _F_
7. Mamie fell from the tree she broke her arm. _R_
8. Martin Luther King led the fight against racial discrimination in the 1950s and 1960s. _S_
9. No, I think I'll stay inside, it's too hot to run. _R_
10. On the far side of the river, chewing on a tree, the beaver. _F_

HINT If a word is a contraction, you should be able to change it into two words and still have a good sentence:

1. It's a girl.   It is a girl. (makes sense)
2. I saw its tail.   I saw it is tail. (does *not* make sense)
3. You're a great player. You are a great player. (makes sense)
4. I like your shirt.   I like you are shirt. (does *not* make sense)

CONTRACTION EXERCISES

A. *Directions:* Turn the italicized words in each sentence into a contraction and write it in the space provided at the end.
   EXAMPLE: I *do not* like sheep. __don't__

1. I *would not* kiss you if you were the last frog on Mars. __wouldn't__
2. *They are* not going to New Zealand this year. __They're__
3. You know *that is* not what I meant. __that's__
4. Maria *will not* finish the book on time. __won't__
5. *I would* love to be a painter some day. __I'd__
6. *They have* lived in this town for years. __They've__
7. Does that mean *you would* see it? __you'd__
8. Bernice *cannot* go on the fact-finding mission to South America. __can't__
9. The astronauts *are not* flying to the moon in May. __aren't__
10. *They will* have to see the ballet another time. __They'll__

B. *Directions:* Rewrite the following contractions as two words.
   EXAMPLE: isn't __is__ __not__

1. wasn't __was__ __not__
2. I'd __I would, I had__
3. you've __you__ __have__
4. shouldn't __should__ __not__
5. I've __I__ __have__
6. let's __let__ __us__
7. didn't __did__ __not__
8. you'd __you would__ __you had__
9. I'm __I__ __am__
10. hasn't __has__ __not__

C. *Directions:* Circle the contractions if the apostrophe is not placed correctly. On the blank next to the word, write the letters that are left out. Put the apostrophe in the right place.
   EXAMPLE: (w'ere) __a__ __we're__

1. they'll _____
2. (are'nt) __o__ __aren't__
3. she's _____
4. they're _____
5. (wo'nt) __o__ __won't__
6. (youv'e) __ha__ __you've__
7. he'll _____
8. shouldn't _____
9. we'll _____
10. (was'nt) __o__ __wasn't__
11. you'll _____
12. (ther'es) __i__ __there's__

To form the possessive of plural nouns that end in *s*, just add an apostrophe to these nouns:

> teachers' cities' writers'

To form the possessive of plural nouns that do *not* end in *s*, add an *'s* to these nouns:

> men's sheep's children's

HINT Before deciding whether to add an apostrophe or an *'s* to a plural noun, first make sure that you have formed the plural of that noun correctly. As you learned in the lesson on nouns, you will need to change some letters when forming the plurals of certain nouns. When forming the possessive plural of a noun, therefore, first change the noun into its plural form and then make the noun possessive:

Singular	Plural	Possessive Plural
boat	boats	boats'
box	boxes	boxes'
thief	thieves	thieves'
baby	babies	babies'
ox	oxen	oxen's
man	men	men's
deer	deer	deer's

POSSESSIVE EXERCISES

A. *Directions:* Change the italicized words into the possessive form of the noun and then rewrite the phrase in the space provided.
   EXAMPLE: the ears *of the dog*   the dog's ears

1. roar *of the ocean* the ocean's roar
2. poems *of John Keats* John Keats's poems
3. call *of the swan* the swan's call
4. speeches *of the politician* the politician's speeches
5. music *of Bach* Bach's music
6. whisper *of the wind* the wind's whisper
7. beauty *of the forest* the forest's beauty
8. life *of Charles* Charles's life
9. cold *of winter* winter's cold
10. hair *of the woman* the woman's hair

B. *Directions:* Fill in the blank in each sentence with the plural possessive form of the noun that appears below the line.
   EXAMPLE: He had five ___days'___ rest at home.
                              day

1. My grandmother belonged to a ___ladies'___ sewing circle.
                                          lady
2. The chorus conductor was pleased with the ___men's___ voices.
                                                      man
3. The ___geese's___ honks woke Matilda from a sound sleep.
             goose
4. The ___children's___ toys lay scattered around the room.
                child
5. All three ___cities'___ airports need to be repaired.
                   city
6. The ___sheep's___ wool is turned into beautiful, warm sweaters.
             sheep
7. The ___Joneses'___ house is really a mansion.
              Jones
8. He looked through the glass window at the ___babies'___ faces.
                                                        baby
9. ___Judges'___ robes are almost always black.
        judge
10. The ___wolves'___ howls sent a tingle up Jennifer's spine.
              wolf

C. *Directions:* Insert apostrophes in the correct places in the following sentences.
   EXAMPLE: I love Jimmy's new bicycle.

1. The two men's shirts were soaked through after the rain.
2. Jane loved all of E.B. White's books.
3. The farmers' market has the best fruit and vegetables in town.
4. I wish I didn't have to go to my uncle's house.
5. Which of the Beatles' records do you own?
6. All three of the doctors' bills were high.
7. The shelves' contents were soon emptied by the thieves.
8. My car's engine fell out at the start of my journey.
9. We passed through the hurricane's eye at 4:00.
10. The musicians' instruments disappeared after their concert.

D. *Directions:* Change the italicized words into the possessive form of the noun and then rewrite the phrase in the space provided.

EXAMPLE: core *of the apple* ___the apple's core___

1. spots *of the ponies* **the ponies' spots**
2. death *of the soldier* **the soldier's death**
3. intelligence *of the women* **the women's intelligence**
4. den *of the foxes* **the foxes' den**
5. hands *of the clock* **the clock's hands**
6. speed *of the cheetah* **the cheetah's speed**
7. depth *of the ocean* **the ocean's depth**
8. mark *of Cain* **Cain's mark**
9. grace *of the eagles* **the eagles' grace**
10. poems *of Robert Burns* **Robert Burns's poems**
11. children *of the McCrumpets* **the McCrumpets' children**
12. bells *of the cathedrals* **the cathedrals' bells**
13. anger *of the mob* **the mob's anger**
14. laughter *of the girls* **the girls' laughter**
15. tears *of the crocodile* **the crocodile's tears**

PLACEMENT OF PUNCTUATION

Use a comma to set off a direct quotation from the rest of the sentence:

1. Gordon said, "I wasn't here yesterday."
2. "I love circuses," Zachary explained.

Always put commas and periods inside the final quotation mark. Place question marks and exclamation points inside the final quotation mark too, *unless* they are *not* part of the actual quotation:

1. "I'm over here," Patricia said.
2. Bill said, "I like to read history books."
3. Gretta asked, "When can I use the car?"
4. "Don't touch that shark!" Bubba screamed.
5. Why did Joanna say, "I believe in equal rights for everyone"? (The question mark is *not* part of the direct quotation, so it goes *outside* the final quotation mark.)

TITLES

In addition to direct quotations, quotation marks are also used to enclose the titles of short stories, short poems, paintings, songs, articles, speeches, chapters, and essays:

"The Lottery" (story)　　　　　"Olympia" (painting)
"The Gettysburg Address" (speech)　　"A Modest Proposal" (essay)

Certain kinds of titles do *not* get enclosed with quotation marks, however. The titles of books, newspapers, magazines, movies, and television shows are underlined instead:

<u>Chicago Tribune</u> (newspaper)　　<u>Life</u> (magazine)
<u>Little Women</u> (book)　　　　　<u>The Sound of Music</u> (movie)

QUOTATION MARKS EXERCISES

A. *Directions:* Insert quotation marks where they are needed in the following sentences. Insert all other punctuation as needed, too. If a sentence is correct already, write a **C** after it.
EXAMPLE: "That's my hat," said Ralph. ____

1. "What did you bring me from Mexico?" Alice asked. ____
2. Ernie heard someone say in the silence, "There goes the ball game."

____

3. Jose said, "See you later," and then walked home. ____

4. June said that she had a stomach ache after eating two pizzas.
   _C_

5. "Bring me the hammer from the basement, please," his mother said.

   ____

6. I was surprised when the dog said, "Fetch me a bone." ____

7. The man said, "Trust me," and winked at Max. ____

8. The girl asked me what we were eating for dinner. _C_

9. "You won't be sorry if you vote for me," the politician promised.

   ____

10. She smiled and answered, "Of course I like country music." ____

B. *Directions:* Rewrite the following indirect quotations as direct quotations and insert quotation marks where they are needed.
   EXAMPLE: Jim said he liked Al's hat.
   "I like your hat," Jim said to Al.

1. Leroy said that a huge blizzard is on the way.
   Leroy said, "A huge blizzard is on the way."

2. Mr. Wiggins told me that I'd better get out of the road.
   Mr. Wiggins told me, "You'd better get out of the road."

3. That strange boy asked me what time it is.
   That strange boy asked me, "What time is it?"

4. Jane said she is going to India for a month.
   Jane said, "I am going to India for a month."

5. I said that I had never seen a purple cat before.
   I said, "I have never seen a purple cat before."

6. The manager asked Frank when he intended to start working.
   The manager asked Frank, "When do you intend to start working?"

C. *Directions:* The following sentences contain a variety of titles. Following the rules for titles, either enclose these in quotation marks or underline them.
   EXAMPLE: Sue played a song called "Freight Train."

1. The <u>Washington Post</u> is one of the best newspapers in the world.
2. One of Sarah's favorite poems is "Nothing Gold Can Stay", by Robert Frost.
3. Jack London wrote a story called "To Build a Fire."
4. <u>War</u> <u>and</u> <u>Peace</u> is a very long novel.
5. "You're the Top" is a Cole Porter song.
6. Humphrey Bogart starred in a movie called <u>Casablanca</u>.
7. Stuart read an article entitled "How to Double Your Savings in a Day."
8. "Sunflowers" is one of Van Gogh's most famous paintings.
9. The name of the chapter is "The River Bank."
10. I read about her in <u>Newsweek</u> magazine.

D. *Directions:* Write a short conversation between two people and insert quotation marks where they are needed.

   _____
   _____
   _____
   _____
   _____
   _____
   _____

   Answers will vary.

13. ADJECTIVES

Read the following sentences. Underline the nouns in each sentence once. Then answer the questions in the spaces provided.

A. Four boys stuffed slimy worms into the big buckets.
   1. *How many* boys? __Four__
   2. *What kind* of worms? __slimy__
   3. *Which* buckets? __big__

B. For heat, tight-fisted Mr. Scrooge daily used two lumps of bituminous coal.
   1. *Which* Mr. Scrooge? __tight-fisted__
   2. *How many* lumps of coal? __two__
   3. *What kind* of coal? __bituminous__

The words you have written in the spaces above modify (describe) other words in three ways. They answer the questions which one? what kind? and how many? *Big* tells which bucket, and *tight-fisted* tells which Mr. Scrooge. *Slimy* tells what kind of worms and *bituminous* tells what kind of coal. *Four* and *two* tell how many boys and how many pieces of coal. Sometimes it is difficult to make a distinction between which one and what kind. *Slimy* could just as easily tell which worms as well as what kind of worms. Both answers would be correct.

Definition
An **adjective** describes or limits a noun or pronoun by telling *which one, what kind,* or *how many.*

Adjectives help you to see objects more clearly. For example, *slimy* lets you imagine the feel of the worms. If you were to say *wriggly* or *whiplike,* you could even begin to see the worms move. In the same way, *tight-fisted* creates the image of a Mr. Scrooge who is miserly and ungenerous. The more vivid and precise the adjectives you use, the clearer the picture you create.

   Now read the italicized sentence below. Underline the nouns once. Then answer the questions in the spaces provided.

In colonial times young girls in needlework schools embroidered many samplers to learn the alphabet and Biblical passages.

1. What words answer *what kind*? __needlework, Biblical__
2. What words do the answers to 1 describe? __schools, passages__
3. What word answers *how many*? __many__
4. What word does the answer to 3 describe? __samplers__
5. What words answer *which one*? __colonial, young__
6. What words do the answer to 5 describe? __times, girls__

What do the words *samplers, schools, passages, times,* and *girls* have in common? Yes, each has an adjective to describe it. Also, each is the same part of speech: a noun. Remember, adjectives always modify nouns or pronouns. Answers to the questions which one and what kind may frequently be interchangeable.

HINTS

A. The adjective is usually located in front of the noun that it modifies.

   Maria put on a *dazzling* hat.

B. Nouns sometimes function as adjectives:

   Helen put on her *baseball* cap.

   In the above sentence, *baseball,* which names something, also describes what kind of cap Helen put on. *Baseball* is a noun functioning as an adjective in this sentence.

C. The three articles (*a, an,* and *the*) always function as adjectives:

   I'll use *the* spoon.

   The tells which spoon the writer will use.

D. Possessive nouns (such as *Henry's, America's,* and *dog's*) and possessive pronouns (*my, mine, your, yours, his, her, hers, its, our, ours, their,* and *theirs*) always function as adjectives:

   Take *Henry's* answers and compare them with *your* answers.

   The adjectives *Henry's* and *your* both tell which answers will be compared.

Practice finding the adjectives in the following sentences. Underline and write *adj.* above each adjective.

1. The *[adj.]* imaginative Anne Shirley helped *[adj.]* shy Matthew and *[adj.]* peevish Marilla discover companionship.
2. Tricky Rumpelstiltskin thought he had trapped the *[adj.]* hapless spinning girl into giving him *[adj.]* her *[adj.]* first-born child.
3. *[adj.]* Some people think *[adj.]* the advertising on *[adj.]* children's television programs traps viewers into wanting too *[adj.]* many toys.

You should have found four adjectives in the first sentence, five in the second sentence, and ~~five~~ four in the last.

ADJECTIVE EXERCISES

A. *Directions:* After each noun, list in the spaces provided three adjectives that precisely and vividly describe it.

EXAMPLE: oatmeal *mushy, beige, lumpy*

1. feather _____
2. diamond _____
3. fish _____
4. sunlight _____
5. school _____
6. fire _____
7. snow _____
8. spiders _____
9. summer _____
10. friend _____

Answers will vary.

B. *Directions:* Change the words listed below into adjectives. Write the answers in the spaces provided.

EXAMPLE: become *becoming*

1. begin **beginning**
2. change **changing or changeable**
3. mercy **merciful**
4. shine **shining or shiny**
5. come **coming**
6. courtesy **courteous**

7. curiosity **curious**
8. who **whose**
9. twelve **twelfth**
10. vigor **vigorous**
11. they **their**
12. ridicule **ridiculous**
13. religion **religious**
14. desire **desirous, desirable, or desiring**
15. disaster **disastrous**
16. eight **eighth**
17. differ **different**
18. imagination **imaginative or imaginary**
19. it **its**
20. mischief **mischievous**

C. *Directions:* Read each sentence. List all the adjectives (except the articles *a*, *an*, and *the*) in the space provided.

EXAMPLE: The humorous Mr. O'Dell told many jokes.
humorous   many

STRANGE BUT TRUE BASEBALL FACTS

1. The first baseball game was played in Hoboken, New Jersey, on June 19, 1846.
   first

2. Baseball's basic rules were not created by Abner Doubleday, but by Alexander J. Cartwright.
   Baseball's, basic

3. Cartwright laid out the present dimensions of the playing field.
   present, playing

4. The first professional team was the Cincinnati Red Stockings.
   first, professional

5. The Red Stockings toured in 1869, and they had an undefeated season.
   undefeated

6. In the late 1900s there were different rules.
   late, different

7. It took nine balls for a walk instead of today's four balls.

nine, today's, four

8. A batter could request a high pitch or a low pitch.

high, low

9. Pitchers made underhand throws and not overhand ones.

underhand, overhand

10. The pitching distance from homeplate to the pitcher's mound was forty-five feet and not the sixty feet and six inches of today.

pitching, pitcher's, forty-five, sixty, six

11. The game of baseball has created unbelievable stories.

unbelievable

12. Baseball has no time clock.

_no_

13. In 1952, in a famous game between the Brooklyn Dodgers and the Cincinnati Reds, a half-inning lasted one hour.

famous, one

14. In that one hour the Dodgers scored fifteen runs in twenty-one times at bat.

that, one, fifteen, twenty-one

15. In another instance Cleveland Indians' pitcher, Eddie Lopat won eleven straight victories against the Yankees.

another, Cleveland Indians', eleven, straight

16. In his next game this streak was broken.

his, next, this

17. A Yankees fan dropped a black cat at Lopat's feet and jinxed him.

Yankees, black, Lopat's

18. He gave up five runs in the first inning, and the Yankees eventually won.

five, first

19. About a hundred years ago, pitcher Fred Goldsmith proved that a curve ball really curves.

hundred, curve

20. He placed three poles in a straight line.

three, straight

21. His pitch skirted the right of the first pole, the left of the second pole, and the right of the third pole.

His, first, second, third

D. *Directions:* Write ten sentences using any adjectives from the right column below to describe a noun from the left column. You may re-use adjectives.

EXAMPLE: voice   scratchy
The scratchy voice travelled through the telephone wire and hit her ear like a rusty knife.

Noun	Adjective
noise	American
teacher	scary
music	wheezy
bus	sixty-five
motorcycle	talking
sight	raspy
goose	eye-dazzling
rainbow	colorful
sandwich	noisy
garden	elderly

1. _____
2. _____
3. _____
4. _____
5. _____
6. _____
7. _____
8. _____
9. _____
10. _____

Answers will vary.

You know much more after reading the second sentence than you do after reading the first. You know **when** Kianga walked to her grandmother's; you know **how** she walked there; and you know **how** she knocked on the door. The adverbs *today*, *briskly*, and *excitedly* give you these extra pieces of information.

HINTS

A. An adverb usually appears next to the verb, adjective, or adverb that it describes.

Kianga walked *extremely hurriedly*, her *brilliantly* colorful dress billowing behind her.

B. Although a word ending in *-ly* is usually an adverb, it can also be an adjective. Some adjectives ending in *-ly* are: ugly, womanly, lovely, stately, and lowly. A few words can function as both adverbs and adjectives:
1. The *fast* train crashed. (adjective)
2. The train went *fast*. (adverb)

C. Nouns often function as adverbs:

Yesterday Sara fell down.

In the sentence above *yesterday* names a thing, a certain day. It also tells when an action took place, so it is a noun functioning as an adverb.

D. *Not* and *never* are always adverbs. They both give negative information: *not* tells how something is done (not at all) and *never* tells when something is done (not ever).

Now that you've been introduced to the adverb, see if you can underline the adverbs in the sentences below:

1. Mary and Bill <u>swiftly</u> and <u>correctly</u> named the specimen.
2. The entire class <u>recently</u> went <u>away</u>.
3. <u>Usually</u> we go <u>quietly</u> to lunch.
4. <u>Today</u> we did <u>not</u> go <u>quietly</u>.

ADVERB EXERCISES

A. *Directions:* Change the words listed below into adverbs. Write the adverbs in the spaces provided.

EXAMPLE: sure   surely

1. new _____ newly
2. immediate _____ immediately
3. late _____ lately
4. accident _____ accidentally
5. able _____ ably
6. beautiful _____ beautifully
7. mystery _____ mysteriously
8. happy _____ happily
9. admirable _____ admirably
10. noisy _____ noisily
11. irritable _____ irritably
12. sensible _____ sensibly
13. ready _____ readily
14. complete _____ completely
15. shy _____ shyly
16. casual _____ casually
17. heavy _____ heavily
18. necessary _____ necessarily
19. true _____ truly
20. intentional _____ intentionally

B. *Directions:* Use *all* the adverbs listed below and write fifteen sentences. Each sentence should have at least one adverb in it. Some sentences will have more than one.

EXAMPLE: yesterday   quickly
Yesterday the giraffe quickly ate all the leaves off the tree.

swiftly	daily	almost	never	really
correctly	up	not	well	yesterday
tenderly	very	today	almost	courageously
promptly	usually	here	there	loudly

_____
_____
_____
_____
_____
_____
_____
_____
_____
_____
_____
_____
_____
_____
_____
_____
_____
_____
_____
_____
_____
_____

Answers will vary.

C. *Directions:* In the following sentences underline each adverb and write *adv.* above it.

EXAMPLE: The events in this exercise *adv.* really happened.

THE BLACK DEATH

1. *adv.* Sometimes an event can *adv.* unexpectedly change the course of history.
2. In the fourteenth century the Black Death *adv.* dramatically changed European society.
3. This plague killed *adv.* approximately one third of Europe's population in four years.
4. A tiny bacterium, *adv.* always found in the stomach of fleas, caused this disease.
5. Small animals *adv.* usually carried the fleas.
6. Black rats *adv.* especially carried these small insects.
7. Italian merchants *adv.* unknowingly brought the plague to Europe from Asia.
8. European merchants and travelers *adv.* very *adv.* quickly spread the disease *adv.* everywhere.
9. City streets were *adv.* almost deserted.
10. Prices soared, shops closed, and necessities became *adv.* extremely scarce.
11. In Paris the plague, at its peak, *adv.* supposedly killed eight hundred people *adv.* daily.
12. Death was *adv.* very common.
13. One witness said, ". . . a dead man was *adv.* then of no more account than a dead goat would be *adv.* today."
14. During the plague, doctors did *adv.* not know the cause of the disease.
15. They *adv.* even blamed the stars, infected winds, and bad smells.
16. After the plague, Europe was *adv.* never the same.
17. European society was *adv.* drastically changed.
18. Europeans related to each other *adv.* differently.
19. The plague *adv.* also changed European governments *adv.* forever.
20. Many historians have *adv.* always considered the Black Death a major turning point in Europe's history.

D. *Directions:* Write a sentence to follow each of the sentence patterns given below. Use articles (*a, an, the*) wherever you need them.

EXAMPLE: ADJ N V

The little bird tweeted.

1. N V ADV

_____

2. ADJ N V ADV

_____

3. ADJ N V ADV

_____

4. ADJ N ADV V

_____

5. ADJ N ADV V ADV

_____

6. ADV ADJ N ADV V ADV

_____

Answers will vary.

Sometimes a preposition may be a group of words:

on account of	in spite of
because of	instead of
according to	out of

Many prepositions can also function as adverbs:

The balloon went *up*.

In this sentence the word *up* answers the question *went, where* and, thus, functions as an adverb. If *up* were a preposition, it would be followed by a noun or pronoun:

The balloon went *up* the *tree*.

HINT A preposition is always found at the *beginning* of a *phrase*, with a *noun* or *pronoun* at the *end* of the phrase:

The ants live *beside* the soap *dish*.

PREPOSITION EXERCISES

A. *Directions:* Underline the prepositions in the following sentences. There can be more than one preposition in each sentence.

EXAMPLE: <u>Around</u> the rock the rascal <u>with</u> the purple patches ran.

1. <u>Underneath</u> the porch the black spiders make huge webs.
2. The small child toddled <u>toward</u> the cookie.
3. The car travelled <u>past</u> the diner.
4. Everyone <u>but</u> Henry carried an instrument.
5. "<u>On</u> the signal, get ready to go," yelled the stern referee. "If you move <u>off</u> your mark, you will be disqualified."
6. <u>Among</u> the trees <u>in</u> the garden, I found the rose <u>with</u> the crimson petals.
7. Many <u>of</u> the hockey players skated <u>without</u> helmets.
8. <u>Over</u> the river and <u>through</u> the woods <u>to</u> grandmother's house we go.
9. There are several warty toads <u>between</u> the rocks <u>near</u> the pond.
10. Will you come <u>to</u> work <u>before</u> school or <u>after</u> classes?

B. *Directions:* Underline the prepositions in the following sentences. There can be more than one preposition in each sentence.

EXAMPLE: The ball rolled <u>into</u> the street.

1. <u>Without</u> helium the balloon will not go <u>above</u> the trees and <u>into</u> the sky.

2. <u>At</u> dawn the weary student finally finished his essay <u>about</u> the life cycle <u>of</u> the common cheese whizzie.
3. Fifteen students will stay <u>in</u> the library <u>until</u> Tuesday to break the All-School Library Sitting Record.
4. Who would want to sit <u>amid</u> all those books, away <u>from</u> pizza and cheeseburgers?
5. No one <u>except</u> those <u>with</u> a dedication <u>beyond</u> my comprehension.
6. <u>At</u> midnight we should go <u>into</u> the library and see these devoted students.
7. <u>Like</u> sentries <u>at</u> their posts, these students always remain awake and alert.
8. <u>Throughout</u> history their fame will spread.
9. "<u>By</u> Jove," Mrs. Fezziwig said. "<u>During</u> the dance you were <u>behind</u> me the entire time, Mr. Fezziwig. Now stay <u>beside</u> me."
10. "<u>Upon</u> my word," replied Mr. Fezziwig. "I will, my dear. This is the best party <u>since</u> the last one."

C. *Directions:* Underline the prepositions in the following sentences. There can be more than one preposition in each sentence.
EXAMPLE: The students stayed <u>for</u> the movie.

TICKET TO FREEDOM

1. <u>Before</u> the Civil War a group <u>of</u> blacks and whites <u>in</u> the North established the Underground Railroad.
2. They used the railroad term *station* <u>for</u> a hiding place and the term *conductor* <u>for</u> men and women helpers.
3. One <u>of</u> the most famous conductors <u>of</u> the Underground Railroad was Harriet Tubman, a former slave.
4. She made nineteen trips <u>into</u> the South <u>during</u> the 1850s and helped more than 300 slaves escape.
5. Most <u>of</u> the people who operated the Underground Railroad were free blacks <u>from</u> the North.
6. Some individual whites provided runaways <u>with</u> food, clothing, directions, and places to hide.
7. Most slaves escaped <u>by</u> themselves <u>without</u> anyone's help.
8. More than 75,000 slaves received help <u>from</u> the Underground Railroad <u>before</u> 1863.
9. This figure was only a small fraction <u>of</u> the total number <u>of</u> blacks <u>in</u> captivity.
10. Abraham Lincoln's Emancipation Proclamation set the majority <u>of</u> blacks free <u>during</u> the Civil War.

D. *Directions:* Use the following combinations of prepositions and prepositional phrases in sentences.
EXAMPLE: to   without her mother
Myra went to the train station without her mother.

1. since   without a computer
_____

2. like   beside the railroad tracks
_____

3. among   into the dark closet
_____

4. below   about the strange bubbles
_____

5. across   near the tattooed lady
_____

6. under   around the race track
_____

7. down   beneath the icy pond
_____

Answers will vary.

E. *Directions:* Put parentheses around each prepositional phrase. Underline the preposition in each phrase.
EXAMPLE: Myra went (<u>to</u> the train station) (<u>without</u> her mother.)

1. Sneezy, Grumpy, and Doc went below (<u>into</u> the mines) and returned (<u>with</u> jewels.)
2. I wanted to go (<u>to</u> the game,) but my friends wanted to stay (<u>at</u> home.)
3. Jake stayed (<u>at</u> the club) (<u>until</u> dinner time.)
4. (<u>Before</u> class) meet me (<u>behind</u> the lockers.)
5. (<u>For</u> the past week) Sarah has come (<u>to</u> class) (<u>without</u> her book.)

A. An interjection usually comes at the beginning of a sentence.
B. An interjection must be followed by either a comma or an exclamation point.

For practice, underline the interjection in each of the following sentences:

1. <u>Wow</u>! This gift is exactly what I wanted.
2. <u>Eureka</u>! Henry decoded the cryptogram.
3. <u>Oh</u>, I thought you didn't want the last piece of cake, so I ate it.

INTERJECTION EXERCISES

A. *Directions:* Underline each interjection.
   EXAMPLE: <u>Gee</u>, I didn't come up with the same answer.

1. <u>Oh, no</u>! I forgot to study for the test!
2. <u>Well</u>, there's no way I'm ever going to pass this one.
3. <u>Hey</u>, why don't they ever ask something I know?
4. <u>Ouch</u>! All this writing is hurting my hand.
5. <u>Oops</u>! My pen just leaked all over my paper.
6. <u>Oh well</u>, that answer was wrong anyway.
7. <u>Aha</u>! I just figured out what the question means.
8. <u>Phooey</u>, I can't remember the answer.
9. <u>Horrors</u>! Time is up, and I just got started.
10. <u>Whew</u>, am I glad that's over.

B. *Directions:* Using either the interjections listed below or others that you know, write a sentence for each of the following situations.

   EXAMPLE: You are surprised that a friend has a motorcycle.
   By Jove! I didn't know you rode a motorcycle.

whew	ouch	help
hurry	my goodness	alas
ah	oh	tsk, tsk
zounds	wow	dear me
eek	aha	eureka
all right	darn	oh, no
shoot	gee whiz	ah me

Answers will vary.

17. CONJUNCTIONS

COORDINATING CONJUNCTIONS

To find out more about conjunctions, read the following sentences and answer the questions in the spaces provided.

A. She was tired and sore.
   1. What words are the adjectives? **tired, sore**
   2. What word joins the adjectives? **and**
B. The dog Sounder limped but moved joyfully toward his master.
   1. What words are the verbs? **limped, moved**
   2. What word joins the verbs? **but**
C. Sherry or Pat will conduct the meeting after school and take the minutes.
   1. What words are the verbs? **will conduct, take**
   2. What word joins the verbs? **and**
   3. What words are the subjects? **Sherry, Pat**
   4. What word joins the subjects? **or**

What words join other words in the above sentences? *And, but,* and *or.* Which words are the conjunctions? Again, *and, but,* and *or.* **Conjunctions** are words that join.

There are three types of conjunctions: **coordinating**, **correlative**, and **subordinating**. We will study only the first two in this lesson. The conjunctions above are called **coordinating conjunctions**. Can you tell why they are called *coordinating* conjunctions?

Definition
Coordinating conjunctions join words or groups of words of equal rank. For now, the term equal rank means words of the same part of speech or function.

Look at sentences A, B, and C above. Adjective is joined with adjective, verb with verb, and noun with noun. In a later lesson you will see how a simple sentence can be joined with another simple sentence.

There are only six coordinating conjunctions: *for, and, nor, but, or,* and *yet.* They are easy to remember. Notice how the first letter of each spells the word *fanboy.*

> For
> And
> Nor
> But
> Or
> Yet

CORRELATIVE CONJUNCTIONS

There is another kind of conjunction. See what you can find out about it from the sentences below. Read the sentences and answer the questions in the spaces provided.

A. Neither Jill nor Jack will be taking the final examination in the head–trauma course.
   1. What words are the subjects? __Jill, Jack__
   2. What words are joining the subjects? __Neither . . . nor__
B. Amy not only sang during the concert but also played the piano.
   1. What words are the verbs? __sang, played__
   2. What words join the verbs? __not only . . . but also__

> **Definition**
> The conjunctions in the above sentences are pairs of words: *neither . . . nor* and *not only . . . but also.* Conjunctions in pairs are called **correlative conjunctions.** Like many relatives (cor*relative*), they choose not to stand alone.

There are five pairs of correlative conjunctions:

> neither . . . nor
> either . . . or
> both . . . and
> not only . . . but (also)
> whether . . . or

Like the coordinating conjunction, the correlative conjunction joins words or groups of words of equal rank.

For practice, underline the coordinating and correlative conjunctions in the sentences below. Remember, correlative conjunctions must be used in pairs. Write the kind of conjunction above each one.

1. The committee cannot decide whether [*corl.*] to buy a VCR or [*corl.*] to rent one.
2. After the performance, she was exhausted but [*coor.*] satisfied.
3. Horace sent invitations to both [*corl.*] the sixth and [*corl.*] seventh grades.
4. Marty and [*coor.*] Pat were absent yesterday but [*coor.*] took the test anyhow.

> **HINT**   *For* can be a preposition as well as a coordinating conjunction:
>
> I made the cake *for* her. (preposition)
> She was proud, *for* she had finished the marathon. (coordinating conjunction)
>
> *Yet* can be an adverb as well as a coordinating conjunction:
>
> Uncle Conrad hasn't arrived *yet.* (adverb)
> The baby was fussy, *yet* cute. (coordinating conjunction)

CONJUNCTION EXERCISES

A. *Directions:* Underline each conjunction in the following sentences. Write *coor.* above each coordinating conjunction and *corl.* over each correlative conjunction.
EXAMPLE: Either [*corl.*] you or [*corl.*] I should call or [*coor.*] write our grandfather.

WOMEN'S STRUGGLE FOR THE VOTE

1. At one time women could neither [*corl.*] vote nor [*corl.*] enjoy other political or [*coor.*] economic rights.
2. In 1848 Elizabeth Cady Stanton and [*coor.*] Lucretia Mott organized a convention on women's rights.
3. As a child, Elizabeth Cady Stanton had heard women complain about men who legally squandered their wives' earnings on liquor or [*coor.*] sold their wives' earnings without consent.
4. As women, Elizabeth Cady Stanton and [*coor.*] Lucretia Mott could attend an anti-slavery meeting but [*coor.*] could not participate.
5. Stanton and [*coor.*] Mott saw these injustices and [*coor.*] decided to hold a convention at Seneca Falls, New York.
6. Both [*corl.*] men and [*corl.*] women attended the convention.

7. Before the convention, neither [*corl.*] Stanton's husband nor [*corl.*] her friends supported giving women the right to vote.

8. In her speech at the meeting, Stanton said that only women could win equal rights, for [*coor.*] they alone could understand the injustices.

9. The convention both [*corl.*] signed a formal "Declaration of Sentiments" and [*corl.*] passed a resolution demanding the right to vote for women.

10. The public's reaction to the women who supported the resolution was either [*corl.*] to ridicule them or [*corl.*] to attack them viciously.

11. The formal "Declaration of Sentiments" not only [*corl. corl.*] copied the Declaration of Independence in style and language but also [*corl. corl.*] declared women's independence from men.

12. The fight for the women's vote was long and [*coor.*] hard, yet [*coor.*] the courageous actions of women like Stanton and [*coor.*] Mott eventually achieved victory.

13. In 1920 women voted for the first time, and [*coor.*] Charlotte Woodard, the only surviving female participant of the Seneca Falls Convention, was among them.

B. *Directions:* Read the following sentences. Use either a coordinating conjunction or correlative conjunction to make each pair or group of sentences into one sentence. Keep the original meaning as much as possible. ✱

EXAMPLE: Mandy rode her bike one day. She rode her skateboard the next.

Mandy rode her bike one day and her skateboard the next day.

1. Bill will go to the dance. Jeff will go to the dance. Winifred will go to the dance.
   <u>Bill, Jeff, and Winifred will go to the dance.</u>

2. King Arthur loved Guinevere. Lancelot loved Guinevere.
   <u>Both King Arthur and Lancelot loved Guinevere.</u>

3. Demeter did not want to give up Persephone. Hades, god of the underworld, did not want to give her up either.
   <u>Neither Demeter nor Hades, god of the Underworld, wanted to give up Persephone.</u>

4. Greedy Midas loved gold. He also loved his daughter.
   <u>Greedy Midas loved gold, but also loved his daughter.</u>

✱ For some sentences there are more than one correct answer. Some answers are more precise or concise than others. The one most concise and most closely preserving the original meaning is given first. Other answers can be found in the back of this book. If students have a variety of answers, the class should discuss why one answer is better than another.

CONJUNCTIONS • 69

5. Echo wanted to talk to Narcissus. She could only repeat what he said. <u>Echo wanted to talk to Narcissus, but could only repeat what he said.</u>

6. Many people do not want to use nuclear energy. They also do not want to use solar energy.
   <u>Many people do not want to use either nuclear or solar energy.</u>

7. Deborah would make a good president. Peter would make a good president. <u>Either Deborah or Peter would make a good president.</u>

8. Zenobia must choose a pet. She can choose a cat. She can choose a dog.
   <u>Zenobia must choose either a cat or a dog.</u>

9. Helen of Troy was the most beautiful woman in the ancient world. She was also the most faithless. <u>Helen of Troy was the most beautiful but the most faithless woman in the ancient world.</u>

10. Sarah gave each person a card. She gave each person a present.
    <u>Sarah gave each person a card and a present.</u>

C. *Directions:* Read the following sentences. Use either a coordinating conjunction or correlative conjunction to make each pair or group of sentences into one sentence. Keep the original meaning as much as possible. ✱

EXAMPLE: Ruby likes movies. Roy likes movies, too.
Both Ruby and Roy like movies.

1. Will you walk the dog now? Will you walk the dog later?
   <u>Will you walk the dog now or later?</u>

2. James had not cleaned his room. James had not completed his homework.
   <u>James had neither cleaned his room nor completed his homework.</u>

3. Go to the store. Buy two quarts of milk, one dozen eggs, and a pound of rice. <u>Go to the store and buy two quarts of milk, one dozen eggs, and a pound of rice.</u>

4. On Tuesday Marion walked to school. On Friday her father drove her. <u>On Tuesday Marion walked to school, but on Friday her father drove her.</u>

5. The manager hired Jill. She was qualified for the job.
   <u>The manager hired Jill, for she was qualified for the job.</u>

6. Have the flowers arrived yet? Have the balloons arrived?
   Have the flowers or the balloons arrived yet?

7. Christopher Columbus set sail to find Asia. He discovered America. *Christopher Columbus set sail to find Asia but discovered America.*

8. We will travel to Washington, D.C. We will visit Williamsburg, too. *We will travel to ^both Washington, D.C. and Williamsburg.*

9. Doctor Watson thought Sherlock Holmes was dead. Sherlock Holmes returned to solve more crimes. Sherlock Holmes continued to pursue Professor Moriarty.
   Doctor Watson thought Sherlock Holmes was dead, but Sherlock Holmes returned to solve more crimes and to pursue Professor Moriarty.

10. Mortimer hadn't cleaned out his locker. Janet hadn't cleaned out hers. *Mortimer hadn't cleaned out his locker, nor had Janet cleaned out hers.*

D. *Directions:* Write a sentence to follow each pattern given below. You may use articles wherever you need them. You may use either type of conjunction for CONJ.
   EXAMPLE: S V CONJ ADJ CONJ ADJ
   She is not only strong but fast.

1. ADJ CONJ ADJ S V.

2. ADJ CONJ ADJ S CONJ S V.

3. ADJ CONJ ADJ S CONJ S V CONJ V.

4. ADJ CONJ ADJ S CONJ S V CONJ V ADV CONJ ADV.

5. INT ADJ CONJ ADJ S CONJ S V CONJ V.

6. CONJ S CONJ S V.

7. S CONJ V CONJ V.

Answers will vary.

18. COMPOUNDS

With conjunctions you can write more interesting and informative sentences. Many sentences together made up of ones—one subject, one verb, one adjective, and so on—would be boring at best. With a conjunction you can join (make **compound**) words or sentences.

This section explains three types of compounds: **compound subjects**, **compound verbs**, and **compound sentences**.

COMPOUND SUBJECTS

Read the following sentences and answer the questions in the spaces provided.

A. Tom and Jerry chased each other throughout the house.
   1. What word is the verb? *chased*
   2. What words are the subjects? *Tom, Jerry*
   3. What word joins the subjects? *and*

B. Either Sakeena, Kim, or Juan will give the speech.
   1. What is the verb phrase? *will give*
   2. What words are the subjects? *Sakeena, Kim, Juan*
   3. What *words* join the subjects? *either, or*

C. In Greek mythology Zeus, Hades, and Poseidon were brothers.
   1. What word is the verb? *were*
   2. What words are the subjects? *Zeus, Hades, Poseidon*
   3. What word joins the subjects? *and*

In the sentences above, more than one subject is present. These subjects are joined by a conjunction. In the first sentence, *and* joins *Tom* and *Jerry*. In the second sentence, *either . . . or* joins *Sakeena*, *Kim*, and *Juan*, and in the third sentence *and* joins *Zeus*, *Hades*, and *Poseidon*. Subjects joined by a conjunction become a compound subject.

> **Definition**
> A **compound subject** is two or more subjects that are joined by a conjunction (either *coordinating* or *correlative*) and share the same verb or verbs.

Now underline the compound subject in the sentence below:

My <u>aunt</u> and <u>uncle</u> have taken care of me since I was two.

COMPOUND VERBS

Remember, a writer can also join two or more verbs with a conjunction. In the following sentences underline the subjects once and the verbs twice. Label the conjunctions *coor.* for coordinating and *corl.* for correlative.

1. <u>Wilma</u> both <u>sang</u> *corl.* and <u>danced</u> *corl.* at the party.
2. The girls' sports <u>class</u> <u>will</u> <u>do</u> warm-up exercises and then <u>play</u> *coor.* softball.

Notice that the subject in each sentence is doing the action of two verbs. *Wilma* does the action of the verbs *sang* and *danced*, and *class* does the action of *do* and *play*. What words join the verbs in each sentence? Again, conjunctions: *both . . . and* in the first sentence; *and* in the second sentence. Verbs joined by a conjunction become a **compound verb**.

> **Definition**
> A **compound verb** is two or more verbs that are joined by a conjunction and share the same subject or subjects.

For practice, underline the conjunctions in each sentence. Put parentheses around the words that each conjunction joins and label them:

1. Harriet <u>not</u> <u>only</u> (washed)ᵛ the car <u>but</u> <u>also</u> (waxed)ᵛ it.
2. <u>Neither</u> (Saul)ˢ <u>nor</u> (Chip)ˢ had seen the movie before.
3. (Myra)ˢ <u>and</u> (Sally)ˢ (came)ᵛ home early from the party <u>and</u> (went)ᵛ to sleep.
4. (Jean,)ˢ (Sam)ˢ <u>and</u> (Dennis)ˢ decided to adopt the skinny dog.

COMPOUND SENTENCES

Use a coordinating conjunction to make one sentence out of each pair of sentences listed below. A comma must be placed before the coordinating conjunction that you add.

1. In the race the motorcycle had the lead. The sports car soon passed it. <u>In the race the motorcycle had the lead, but the sports car soon passed it.</u>

2. Mrs. Valdez was happy. She had just created the world's largest anchovy pizza. <u>Mrs. Valdez was happy, for she had just created the world's largest anchovy pizza.</u>
3. The delivery man dropped off the package at the store. The storekeeper unwrapped it. <u>The delivery man dropped off the package at the store, and the storekeeper unwrapped it.</u>

You have just turned six simple sentences into three **compound sentences**.

> **Definition**
> Two or more simple sentences (independent clauses) joined by a coordinating conjunction are called a **compound sentence**.

As you've learned already, an independent clause is another name for a simple sentence: it can stand by itself, be independent, and make sense.

When you join simple sentences with conjunctions, you create more interesting sentences. Compound sentences break up the boredom of one simple sentence after another and another followed by another and so on throughout a paragraph or story.

In a compound sentence you can show more precisely how one idea relates to another by using the conjunction that best expresses the relationship between these ideas. Look again at the sentences at the beginning of this section. You'll find that some conjunctions make the meaning clearer than others.

The motorcycle had the lead in the race, but the sports car soon passed it.

The sentence above makes more sense than:

The motorcycle had the lead in the race, and the sports car soon passed it.

The first rewrite shows the surprise of the action. When you read about the action in the first part, you don't expect the action of the second part. *But* and *yet* are coordinating conjunctions that emphasize the unexpected or contrast the different. The conjunction *and* merely joins the two sentences as if they were equal in excitement. The second rewrite makes the action sound commonplace and humdrum.

COMPOUND EXERCISES

A. *Directions:* In the following sentences change the plural subjects to compound subjects. Try using three or more subjects in some sentences.
EXAMPLE: They went early to the concert to obtain good seats.
James, Janine, and Jerry went early to the concert to obtain good seats.

1. We went to the game early to set up the refreshment stand.
   _____

2. The teams had early practices and then discussed strategy for the next day's games.
   _____

3. Spring flowers always bring thoughts of summer vacation.
   _____

4. They desperately wanted to go on a three-day canoe trip on the Allagash with their friends.
   _____

5. The musical groups appeared in the stadium for the benefit concert.
   _____

6. The dogs barked loudly, and Ms. Winter quickly let them out.
   _____

7. Some cars need frequent tune-ups, but others can go for months without one.
   _____

8. Holidays are more than welcome to all students.
   _____

9. Authors write so readers can understand the characters and perhaps understand themselves better.
   _____

10. Birds make good pets for people who like to change newspapers, but fish are quieter.
   _____

11. Radio stations often play only a few songs from an album, and they play them over and over.
   _____

Answers will vary.

12. Today's movies sometimes comment on life as well as offer entertainment.
   _____

13. Many sports are shown on T.V.
   _____

14. His clothing was wrinkled, and his shoes were untied. (What other change must you make in this sentence?)
   _____

15. The jury has voted to order pizza with pepperoni but without mushrooms. (What other change must you make in this sentence?)
   _____
Answers will vary.

B. *Directions:* In the following sentences insert a compound verb in the spaces provided.
EXAMPLE: The wolf <u>huffed and puffed</u> but it did no good.

1. Everyone _____ at the party.
2. In the movie all of the actors _____.
3. Scout, Jem, and Dill _____ all summer long.
4. Teachers always _____.
5. When catching a unicorn, make sure you not only _____ but also _____.
6. Friends should _____ thoughtfully but shouldn't _____.
7. The detective will either _____ or _____.
8. During the game, the fans _____.
9. After the heavy rains, the rivers and streams _____.
10. Before a test, I _____.
Answers will vary.

C. *Directions:* Read the following sentences. Underline the compound subjects once and the compound verbs twice.
EXAMPLE: The windows <u>rattled and banged</u> in the wind.

ACHIEVEMENTS OF EARLY LATIN AMERICAN INDIANS

1. In the 1500s Spanish explorers <u>invaded</u> and <u>conquered</u> the Indian tribes of Latin America.
2. European <u>rulers</u> and <u>clergy</u> believed that the Indian societies were primitive, uncivilized, and inferior.
3. In truth, the <u>Mayans</u>, <u>Aztecs</u>, and <u>Incas</u> often surpassed the Europeans in many areas.

4. Mayan mathematicians <u>invented</u> and <u>used</u> a superior mathematical system.

5. Their <u>discovery</u> and <u>use</u> of the zero allowed them to calculate into the millions.

6. The <u>Mayans</u> and <u>Aztecs</u> developed a 365-day calendar.

7. Neither the <u>French</u> nor the <u>Spanish</u> had developed a more accurate calendar.

8. The <u>population</u> and <u>size</u> of the Aztec capital was substantially larger than any Spanish city of its day.

9. The <u>Aztecs</u> of Mexico and the <u>Incas</u> of Peru ruled empires larger than most European states.

10. Over 60,000 visitors <u>shopped</u> daily and <u>browsed</u> in the shops of the Aztec capital.

11. The palace of the Aztec emperor <u>had</u> three hundred rooms and <u>was</u> larger than the palace of the French king.

12. The dry <u>climate</u> and steep <u>terrain</u> of the Incan empire did not prevent growing enough food to feed its 12,000,000 inhabitants.

13. The <u>technique</u> of terraced farming and a <u>network</u> of irrigation canals made Incan farmers as advanced as farmers anywhere in Europe.

D. *Directions:* Read the following sentences. Use a conjunction to make each pair of simple sentences into a compound sentence. Use the conjunction that makes the best relationship between the sentences. Don't forget to use a comma before a coordinating conjunction in a compound sentence. *

EXAMPLE: The cat can run very fast. The dog can run faster.
    The cat can run very fast, but the dog can run faster.

AN AMERICAN LEGEND

1. Folk stories often reveal much about a country. American tall tales are no exception. *Folk stories often reveal much about a country, and American tall tales are no exception.*

2. Our tall tales reveal the constant movement of our pioneer forefathers. They also reveal valued human characteristics. *Our tall tales reveal not only the constant movement of our pioneer forefathers, but also valued human characteristics.*

3. Paul Bunyan is a famous American folk hero. He was born in Nova Scotia, Canada. *Paul Bunyan is a famous American folk hero, but he was born in Nova Scotia, Canada.*

4. His parents were French fisherfolk. His name was originally Paul Bonjean. *His parents were French fisherfolk, and his name was originally Paul Bonjean.*

* See note on p. 69.

5. At birth Paul weighed over fifty pounds. All the cows in the neighborhood gave their milk for Paul's food. *At birth Paul weighed over fifty pounds, and all the cows in the neighborhood gave their milk for his food.*

6. His parents were very worried. Paul outgrew everything. *His parents were very worried, for Paul outgrew everything.*

7. His clothes did not fit. His cradle did not fit. *His clothes and his cradle did not fit.*

8. An unused mainsail became his diapers. The largest ship's hull in the China trade became his cradle. *An unused mainsail became his diapers, and the largest ship's hull in the China trade became his cradle.*

9. Paul was extremely bright. He had problems in school. *Paul was extremely bright, but he had problems in school.*

10. He could fit only one letter on each page. His geography book had to be carried by a team of oxen. *He could fit only one letter on each page, and his geography book had to be carried by a team of oxen.*

11. One day he accidentally sat on his lunch box. When he opened it, he discovered his first invention, hamburger. *One day he accidentally sat on his lunch box, but when he opened it, he discovered his first invention, hamburger.*

12. Paul left school. He had to choose his career. *Paul left school, for he had to choose a career.*

13. He tried fishing, hunting, and trapping. They were too easy. *He tried fishing, hunting, and trapping, but they were too easy.*

14. He retreated to a cave. There he met his lifelong companion, Babe. *He retreated to a cave and there met his lifelong companion, Babe.*

15. Babe, an ox as big as Paul, was a very strange shade of blue. As a calf she had been abandoned in the deepest snow on record and had never lost the color of that deep chill. *Babe was an ox as big as Paul and a very strange shade of blue, for as a calf she had been abandoned in the deepest snow on record and had never lost the color of that deep chill.*

16. One day Babe knocked down a tree. Then Paul knew he was to invent logging to clear the land for American pioneers. *One day Babe knocked down a tree, and then Paul knew he was to invent logging to clear the land for American pioneers.*

17. Nothing could stop Paul. Thirst did not stop him. Heat did not stop him. *Neither thirst nor heat could stop him.*

18. When Babe was thirsty, Paul dug a drinking hole that is now the famous geyser, Old Faithful. When Paul became hot, he walked in a river and made the Grand Canyon. *When Babe was thirsty, Paul dug a drinking hole that is now the famous geyser Old Faithful, and when Paul became hot, he walked in a river and made the Grand Canyon.*

19. This ingenious American folk hero was bigger than life. American settlers saw their new land as endless and wanted to be as creative and sturdy as Paul Bunyan. *This American folk hero was bigger than life and ingenious, for American settlers saw their new land as endless and wanted to be as creative and sturdy as Paul Bunyan.*

E. *Directions:* Underline each conjunction in the following sentences and put parentheses around the items it joins. Label the items *s* for subject, *v* for verb, or *sen.* for sentence.
   EXAMPLE: Jules and Jim went swimming.
   (Jules)^s <u>and</u> (Jim)^s went swimming.

   1. Nancy (took a)^v shower <u>and</u> (washed)^v her hair.
   2. Bob Cratchit (looked)^v forward to Christmas <u>and</u> (celebrated)^v with much glee.
   3. In summer, students (rest)^v from schoolwork <u>and</u> (participate)^v in other activities.
   4. (Superman is a traditional hero in many ways)^SEN. <u>but</u> (he was born in outer space.)^SEN.
   5. Were either (you)^s <u>or</u> (Isabel)^s at the game last night?
   6. At the zoo we (saw)^v many animals <u>but</u> (liked)^v the panda most.
   7. (Margaret Mitchell is best known for her book *Gone with the Wind.*)^SEN. <u>for</u> (she wrote no other novels.)^SEN.
   8. (Bilbo)^s (Gandalf)^s <u>and</u> twelve (dwarves)^s went off to slay the dragon.
   9. (Anne Frank was killed in a Nazi concentration camp during World War II,)^SEN. <u>but</u> (her spirit lives on in her diary.)^SEN.
   10. The clean-up committee (will take)^v down the decorations, (put)^v away the chairs, <u>and</u> (wash)^v the floor.

F. *Directions:* Underline each conjunction in the following sentences and put parentheses around the items it joins. Label the items *s* for subject, *v* for verb, or *sen.* for sentence.
   EXAMPLE: Rory (ran)^v to town <u>and</u> (bought)^v a shirt.

   1. <u>Both</u> the (teachers)^s <u>and</u> the (librarians)^s suggested good books to the class.
   2. (No one recommended *Death Be Not Proud*)^SEN. <u>yet</u> (I found it hard to put down.)^SEN.
   3. Myra (read)^v *To Kill a Mockingbird* <u>and</u> especially (liked)^v the surprise ending.
   4. Many students (enjoyed)^v the rebellious Huck Finn <u>and</u> then (read)^v *The Adventures of Tom Sawyer.*
   5. (Sam)^s <u>and</u> his (brother)^s like animal stories.
   6. (Sam is reading *Sounder*)^SEN. <u>and</u> (his brother is reading *The Incredible Journey.*)^SEN.
   7. (Many of us read books recently published)^SEN. <u>yet</u> (others picked up books published a long time ago.)^SEN.
   8. (The teachers like us to read old-fashioned books)^SEN. <u>but</u> (we sometimes like to read books about teenagers today.)^SEN.
   9. Many books (tell)^v about teenagers today <u>and</u> (help)^v us understand ourselves better.
   10. There are many (novels)^s <u>and</u> short (stories)^s about teen-agers in the Young Adult section in the library.

19. SUBJECT AND VERB AGREEMENT

Read the following sentences. Find the error in each one. Correct the error in the space provided.

1. The songs contains many harmonious guitar parts.
   contain

2. My father have shown me how to throw a curve ball.
   has

3. Both Ms. Peabody's class and Mr. Wong's class eats lunch at noon and then goes to music class.
   eat, go

These sentences don't sound right. Your ear probably hears the errors even if you don't know the name for them. What parts don't fit together? If you're having trouble finding the errors, go back and underline each verb twice and each subject once. What do you discover?

In the first sentence the subject mentions more than one song (*songs*) but the verb, *contains*, is singular.

In the second sentence the subject, *father*, is singular, but the verb, *have shown*, is plural.

In the last sentence there are two subjects, *Ms. Peabody's class* and *Mr. Wong's class*, joined by a coordinating conjunction. Like an addition sign (+), a coordinating conjunction adds these two subjects together to make a plural. The error? Each verb, *eats* and *goes*, is singular.

Definition
A verb must **agree** with its subject in number. If the subject is singular, the verb must be singular. If the subject is plural, then the verb must be plural.

The two chickens have decided not to lay eggs.

The farmer has decided to serve roast chicken.

In the sentences above, the plural subject, *chickens*, takes a plural verb, *have decided*, while the singular subject, *farmer*, takes a singular verb, *has decided*.

Subjects and verbs must agree in other ways that your ear can also probably hear. In later grammar books you will study other forms of agreement.

HINTS

A. If a compound subject is joined by *and*, the verb is plural. Remember, the *and* acts as an addition sign:

   Jean and Ed are cousins.

B. If the compound verb is joined by *or* or *nor*, the verb agrees with the nearest subject:
   1. Neither the coach nor the *players think* the team will lose.
   2. Neither the players nor the *coach thinks* the team will lose.
   3. Neither he nor *I am* ready for the audition.

C. Be careful not to confuse the subject of a sentence with the noun or pronoun that follows a preposition:
   1. One of these stories *is* a lie. (**not** *are*)
   2. The ears on that rabbit *are* huge. (**not** *is*)

For practice, write the correct verb for each subject in the space provided:

1. The picture (hangs, hang) on the first floor of the museum.   _hangs_
2. The picture of the cottages (hangs, hang) on the first floor of the museum.   _hangs_
3. The bird watchers quietly (stalks, stalk) the gray-tipped chalk eater.   _stalk_
4. Either my father or brothers (has packed, have packed) my lunch.   _have packed_

SUBJECT AND VERB AGREEMENT EXERCISES

A. *Directions:* Some verbs and subjects are listed below. For each verb write a subject in the space provided that agrees with the verb. For each subject write a verb in the space provided that agrees with the subject.
   EXAMPLE: walks _____Jerry_____
            birds _____fly_____

   1. Henry and Terry _____
   2. _____ doesn't
   3. Many of the people _____
      Answers will vary.

4. Either the blue or the gray one _____

5. _____ crept

6. oxen _____

7. class _____

8. participants _____

9. _____ go

10. Either you or they _____

B. *Directions*: Some verbs and subjects are listed below. For each verb write a subject in the space provided that agrees with the verb. For each subject write a verb in the space provided that agrees with the subject.

EXAMPLE: had seen *many lifeguards*

1. _____ don't

2. _____ have been

3. sheep _____

4. _____ were

5. women _____

6. Either the club members or the president _____

7. Several dancers _____

8. Neither the team nor the spectators _____

9. _____ am

10. Both you and I _____
    Answers will vary.

C. *Directions:* Circle the correct verb in the parentheses.

EXAMPLE: Several boys (has tried, (have tried)) out for the team.

MYSTERIOUS MONSTER

1. Many people in the United States and Canada (believes /(believe)) in the existence of Bigfoot.

2. Some Indian tribes (calls /(call)) this apelike creature Sasquatch.

3. One hundred and fifty years ago, the first report of a "wild man" ((was)/ were) published in a New Orleans newspaper.

4. Since then over one thousand sightings of Bigfoot (has /(have)) been reported.

5. Each one of these reports ((describes)/ describe) a large, furry creature of some sort with broad shoulders and long arms.

6. Red or glowing eyes, a strong, unpleasant odor, and an upright walk on two feet (is /(are)) characteristics often mentioned.

7. The height of the creature ((is)/ are) said to range from seven to ten feet.

8. Its tracks (measures /(measure)) seventeen inches long and seven inches wide.

9. One of the most interesting claims of Bigfoot's existence ((is)/ are) found in a short movie.

10. In the movie, scenes supposedly (shows /(show)) a female Bigfoot.

11. The blurred images and the camera's distance from the creature (makes /(make)) it impossible to see clearly.

12. People looking at the film (disagrees /(disagree)) about the subject.

13. Many people (says /(say)) it is a female Bigfoot, and others (says / (say)) it isn't.

14. A few scientists (thinks /(think)) that Bigfoot may be a distant relative of an apelike animal.

15. Theories (states /(state)) that this apelike creature migrated during prehistoric times from Asia to North America.

16. Most people, however, (remains /(remain)) unconvinced that Bigfoot exists.

17. Neither scientists nor anyone else ((seems)/ seem) able to explain the many sightings of Bigfoot.

18. Maybe this creature really ((does)/ do) exist.

19. There (is /(are)) no other explanations.

20. What (is /(are)) your thoughts about Bigfoot?

D. *Directions:* In each sentence choose the verb that agrees with the subject. Write your answer in the space provided.

EXAMPLE: Several girls also (has tried, have tried) out. *have tried*

1. The small boy (walks, walk) to kindergarten by himself.
   walks

2. The science class (doesn't, don't) want to go to the museum by bus. _doesn't_

3. My mother and I (hasn't, haven't) seen that movie.
   haven't

4. Neither Nicholas nor Katharine (has, have) left.
   has

5. Both Doug and Mary (has been, have been) seen there.
   have been

6. Either Dan or Yoni (needs, need) extra study time.
   needs

7. People in the bus (leaves, leave) by the rear door.
   leave

8. Neither you nor I (am, are) ready to audition.
   _am_

9. Both of us (was, were) nervous at the dance.
   were

10. My sweat pants (slips, slip) down during exercises.
    slip

11. Where (has, have) all the doughnuts gone? _have_

12. There (is, are) only two possible answers. _are_

13. One of the cows (has, have) slipped through the fence.
    has

14. A member of the band always (helps, help) set up the equipment.
    helps

15. Three of the gang (seems, seem) uninterested in the concert.
    seem

16. Marilyn's overalls (was, were) covered with dirt.
    were

17. The teachers and the class (sees, see) a filmstrip once a week.
    see

18. Neither the teachers nor the class (misses, miss) the filmstrips.
    misses

19. The horses in the barn (doesn't, don't) move.
    don't

20. Every one of her flowers (grows, grow) large and fragrant.
    grows

20. COMPREHENSIVE EXERCISES

PARTS OF SPEECH

A. *Directions:* Write the correct part of speech above each underlined word. If a noun functions as either an adjective or an adverb, label it according to its function.

N for noun	ADV for adverb
PRO for pronoun	PREP for preposition
V for verb	CONJ for conjunction
ADJ for adjective	INT for interjection

EXAMPLE: The United States Constitution changed <u>the</u> [ADJ] history <u>not only</u> [CONJ] of the United States <u>but also</u> [CONJ] of the world.

THE MAKING OF THE U.S. CONSTITUTION

1. In May, 1787, <u>fifty-five</u> [ADJ] delegates from twelve states met at the Constitutional Convention in Philadelphia to discuss replacing the <u>Articles</u> [N] of Confederation.

2. The Articles of Confederation were the rules <u>of</u> [PREP] government under which the colonies <u>had fought</u> [V] the Revolutionary War.

3. These Articles brought <u>together</u> [ADV] thirteen independent colonies into <u>a</u> [ADJ] "firm league of friendship" to fight England.

4. After the Revolutionary War, the fragile union of the colonies began to fall <u>apart</u> [ADV], and the Articles of Confederation could not hold <u>them</u> [PRO] together.

5. Each state government had more <u>power</u> [N] than the Congress, and each state felt it was more important than its neighboring states <u>or</u> [CONJ] even the United States itself.

6. Each state <u>could</u> [V] make <u>its</u> [PRO or ADJ] own money, and some states printed so much paper money that it was almost worthless.

7. To help raise money, some states <u>taxed</u> [V] people just for crossing the state line <u>from</u> [PREP] another state.

8. In 1787 the unexpected and violent rebellion of Daniel Shays, <u>a</u> [ADJ]
former Massachusetts captain <u>in</u> [PREP] the Revolutionary Army, finally
forced many leaders to review the Articles.

9. Shays <u>collected</u> [V] an army of desperate, debt-ridden farmers to pro-
test the seizure of farms, but ultimately this small group of armed
men prevented the Supreme Court <u>from</u> [PREP] meeting in Springfield,
Massachusetts.

10. In order to prevent the <u>capture</u> [N] of the Federal arsenal, the Congress
of the United States <u>frantically</u> [ADV] voted to raise money for an army.

11. <u>Alas</u> [INT], twelve of the thirteen states ignored the request for money,
and <u>finally</u> [ADV] wealthy men from Massachusetts gave the money to
raise the army that defeated Shays.

12. The Congress was powerless <u>not only</u> [CONJ] to raise money for an army
against Shays, but also to collect taxes for any armed defense
<u>during</u> [PREP] the war.

13. Many of the <u>country's</u> [ADJ or N] leaders feared that soon thirteen independent countries <u>would exist</u> [V], so in 1787 many became delegates to
the Constitutional Convention in Philadelphia.

14. The delegates elected George Washington as the leader of this
convention, and <u>he</u> [PRO] skillfully guided the <u>often</u> [ADV] heated discussion.

15. <u>Throughout</u> [PREP] the hot, humid summer convention delegates de-
bated the value of a central government's authority versus the
value of each <u>state's</u> [ADJ or N] authority.

16. Finally, on <u>September</u> [N] 17, <u>1787</u> [N], all the delegates signed the Constitution of the United States.

17. <u>Under</u> [PREP] the new Constitution the states kept some powers, <u>but</u> [CONJ]
others were given only to the central government.

18. The Constitution created a central government <u>with</u> [PREP] three equal
branches: the <u>legislative</u> [ADJ], the executive, and the judicial.

19. The Constitution granted power to each branch to check any of
the other three branches, so <u>no</u> [ADJ] authority <u>had</u> [V] all the power.

20. The Constitution of the United States established <u>for</u> [PREP] the first time
in history a government created by a nation's citizens and <u>not</u> [ADV] by
those who governed.

B. *Directions:* Write the correct part of speech above each underlined
word. If a noun or pronoun functions as either an adjective or an
adverb, label it according to its function.

N for noun   ADV for adverb
PRO for pronoun   PREP for preposition
V for verb   CONJ for conjunction
ADJ for adjective   INT for interjection

EXAMPLE: <u>The</u> [ADJ] story of Daedalus and Icarus <u>is</u> [V] a lesson in how to
behave.

DAEDALUS AND ICARUS: A GREEK MYTH

1. The myth of <u>Daedalus</u> [N] and Icarus reveals the most important value
of <u>ancient</u> [ADJ] Greek society.

2. The story begins with Daedalus, <u>an</u> [ADJ] extremely gifted craftsman in
all <u>things</u> [N] scientific and <u>artistic</u> [ADJ].

3. Every ruler in Greece and the surrounding kingdoms wanted this
<u>master's</u> [ADJ or N] services, but Daedalus desired <u>only</u> [ADV] the freedom to wan-
der.

4. One of <u>his</u> [ADJ or PRO] journeys brought <u>him</u> [PRO] to the Mediterranean island of
Crete.

5. King Minos <u>asked</u> [V] Daedalus to plan for the king the most beautiful
palace <u>ever</u> [ADV] built.

6. Daedalus <u>obliged</u> [V] the king and designed a palace <u>with</u> [PREP] a fantastic
labyrinth (maze) <u>underneath</u> [ADV].

7. King Minos saw the finished palace and said to Daedalus, "<u>By</u> [INT]
<u>Zeus</u>! <u>Never</u> [ADV] has such a beautiful palace <u>been seen</u> [V] by <u>either</u> [CONJ] men
<u>or</u> [CONJ] gods."

8. Daedalus lived <u>on</u> [PREP] Crete, in the <u>king's</u> [ADJ or N] <u>favor</u> [N], until one fateful day.

9. Ariadne, King Minos's daughter, was <u>almost</u> [ADV] sick with love <u>for</u> [PREP]
Theseus, a Greek hero trapped in the labyrinth.

10. <u>She</u> [PRO] asked Daedalus how Theseus <u>might</u> [V] escape, and Daedalus
told her.

11. Theseus escaped and took <u>Adriadne</u> [N] with <u>him</u> [PRO].

12. King Minos was angry <u>beyond</u> [PREP] measure and imprisoned Daedalus
and <u>his</u> [ADJ or PRO] son, Icarus, in the labyrinth.

13. Daedalus and Icarus <u>easily</u> [ADV] escaped from the labyrinth, but how
<u>were</u> [V] they to leave the island?

14. The **[ADJ]** wily Daedalus built two sets of wings from feathers and wax so he **[CONJ]** and his son could fly **[PREP]** over the sea.

15. "**[INT]** Well, my son," said Daedalus. "These wings will help to set **[PRO]** us free, **[CONJ]** but do **[ADV]** not fly close to either the sun or the sea or you **[V]** will surely perish."

16. Icarus began their flight **[PREP]** by obediently trailing his father, but the ecstasy of soaring weightlessly **[PREP]** through the air proved **[ADV]** too much.

17. He flew closer and **[ADV]** closer to the sun, and his wings melted **[PREP]** into useless lumps.

18. Cursing his own invention, grief-stricken Daedalus buried his most beloved son on the island that still **[V]** bears his son's name.

19. Daedalus sadly went **[PREP]** on his way to escape the murderous **[N]** anger of Minos.

20. To the Greeks this story taught the lesson of **[ADV]** never going **[PREP]** to extremes but of doing all things in moderation.

C. *Directions:* Write the correct part of speech above each underlined word. If a noun or pronoun functions as either an adjective or an adverb, label it according to its function.

N for noun	ADV for adverb
PRO for pronoun	CONJ for conjunction
V for verb	PREP for preposition
ADJ for adjective	INT for interjection

EXAMPLE: **[ADV]** There are many types **[PREP]** of sports.

1. The referee signaled a penalty of **[ADJ]** fifteen yards **[PREP]** for holding.

2. Julius tentatively placed his foot in the only **[N]** toehold on the **[ADV]** almost sheer rock face.

3. **[PREP]** Before the competition Gladys practiced **[ADV]** over and over **[PRO or ADV]** her figure eights, **[CONJ]** for she wanted to win the **[ADJ]** ice skating championship.

4. Bobbing almost aimlessly in the **[ADJ]** white water, Sabrina's canoe barely made **[PRO]** it **[PREP]** through the deadly rapids.

5. The baseball hit the wall **[PREP]** in left **[N]** field, but Jim quickly **[V]** fielded it and made a double play.

6. Larry had **[V]** dribbled the ball deftly down center court and made the basket.

7. Sweat poured **[PREP]** over Jill's brow, **[CONJ]** yet she dug her toes **[PREP]** into the cinders and placed her heels in the starting block.

8. She tried to block the kick, but the ball went **[PREP]** between the **[ADJ or N]** goalie's legs.

9. During the frantic **[N]** pace of the aerobic exercises, Jack felt his heart pounding **[PREP]** throughout his body.

10. Jenna raised her stick and **[V]** drove the ball **[PREP]** toward the right wing.

11. **[ADJ]** Eager to show his accomplishments, Jeff **[V]** chalked his hands and headed confidently to the **[ADJ]** parallel bars.

12. **[ADV]** Never having played **[ADJ]** this position, Mike nervously skated **[PREP]** after the puck.

13. The coxswain rhythmically chanted, and the four rowers **[ADV]** vigorously rowed in **[N]** unison.

14. Greg walked to the **[N]** end of the diving board, poised himself on the **[N]** edge, and **[ADV]** then dove into the water.

15. **[PREP]** From the top of the slope, the ski run **[V]** seemed to stretch almost to the **[ADJ]** next mountain, **[CONJ]** yet Bob was determined to get to the **[N]** bottom.

16. Tired beyond **[N]** endurance, Maria turned the corner and jogged **[ADV or N]** home.

17. **[ADJ]** The sail began to luff, **[CONJ]** for John had headed the boat **[ADV]** away from the wind.

18. As the bicyclist rode **[PREP]** up the hill, he **[V]** shifted gears and pedaled **[ADV]** faster.

19. **[INT]** Oh, no! The horse did **[ADV]** not clear the fence, and the rider is down.

20. Gillian grabbed the bar and waited for the wind to tug her **[ADJ]** hang glider into open air.

SENTENCES

A. *Directions:* Write the subject(s) of each of the following sentences in the space provided at the end.

EXAMPLE: The dragon devoured St. George. ___*dragon*___

1. Maxwell drank every drop of his coffee. ___Maxwell___

2. Yesterday Mr. Proctor gambled all his money and lost. ___Mr. Proctor___

3. The crest of the wave swept Chauncey Colgate off his surfboard.
___crest___

4. The king's favorite burgers came from the corner cafe.
___burgers___

5. On Monday the police found the janitor in a drum.
___police___

6. The scope of the investigation takes my breath away.
___scope___

7. The powerful surf dragged the washing machine out with the tide. ___surf___

8. My three sons did a fantastic job on the bathroom walls.
___sons___

9. This morning Melvin and Bess pledged to wax the old table.
___Melvin, Bess___

10. The dirty dishes cascaded to the floor. ___dishes___

11. The removal of the garbage bags made them all glad.
___removal___

12. Did Rose really leave her cereal bowl on the post?
___Rose___

13. The Quakers next door raise hay and oats. ___Quakers___

14. Peter skipped his peanut butter sandwich today.
___Peter___

15. Sal, Tad, and Fred drank their juice with the spray of the ocean in their faces. ___Sal, Tad, Fred___

16. The weather in Canada was dry all summer. ___weather___

17. Morton likes lots of salt on his potatoes. ___Morton___

18. Why will there be no soup at Mrs. Campbell's wedding reception?
___soup___

19. Every day Duncan eats four doughnuts for breakfast.
___Duncan___

20. Scott sneezed and reached for another tissue.
___Scott___

B. *Directions:* In the space at the end of each group of words, write **F** if it is a fragment, **R** if it is a run-on, or **S** if it is a sentence.
EXAMPLE: Chuck ran to school. _S_

1. Singing all those songs again at the top of his lungs. _F_
2. Even if we were going to the North Pole on a camel. _F_
3. Mt. Rushmore is located in South Dakota. _S_
4. Tom won the poetry award, that's why he's smiling. _R_
5. When the baby saw his mother. _F_
6. Yes, I know exactly what I'm doing. _S_
7. Tony sprained his ankle on the hike, it really hurt. _R_
8. Meeting the governor after the banquet. _F_
9. Driving at high speeds frightened Carter. _S_
10. Gracie was nervous about the biology quiz. _S_
11. Jake looked in the open window then he climbed inside. _R_
12. In the middle of the night rushing through the tall trees. _F_
13. Although she admitted she hadn't seen the circus before. _F_
14. John Steinbeck wrote *The Grapes of Wrath*. _S_
15. Scared that he would have to take his little brother. _F_
16. We spent the day hiking my feet ached that night. _R_
17. Stan left the house that morning, consequently, he missed the fire.
_R_
18. Into the lake, feeling the cold water on his shoulders. _F_
19. The Russian serfs were freed in 1863. _S_
20. Since Rita ran in the marathon, this past summer. _F_

C. *Directions:* Revise the following groups of words into one *or* two complete sentences. You may have to add words, capitalize letters, or change or insert punctuation.
EXAMPLE: He sat down she sat down next to him.
He sat down. She sat down next to him.

1. On the top of the refrigerator in the kitchen

_____

2. Hank played the guitar his sister played the fiddle

_____

3. If Beth wins the lottery tonight

_____

4. The wailing of the ambulance's siren

_____

5. Ted watched television for eight hours his brain turned to mush

_____

6. Julie eyed the shark with suspicion then she decided to leave the water

_____

7. Spinning on top of the table

_____

8. Bilbo Baggins is the hero of *The Hobbit* it is a wonderful book

_____

9. After Professor Blake finished his brilliant lecture

_____

10. Over the fence and through the field the horse

_____

11. Why are you going home, I said I'm sorry

_____

12. When Terry saw the pumpkins covered with frost

_____

13. Henry James was a novelist, William James was a philosopher

_____

14. During the hurricane many of the houses

_____

15. Rudyard Kipling was born in India then he went to school in England

_____

Answers will vary.

D. *Directions:* Depending on what type of sentence it is, write *simple* or *compound* in the space after each of the following sentences.
EXAMPLE: Biff loves spaghetti. _____*simple*_____

1. Joan won the race, but she cheated. ___compound___
2. The sailor saw the lighthouse flash again. ___simple___
3. Len bought the coat and paid in cash. ___simple___
4. The Germans won some battles, yet they lost the war.
   ___compound___
5. Betsy missed first base, so the umpire called her out.
   ___compound___
6. Leo and Nancy saw a flying saucer. ___simple___

7. Thirty penguins escaped from the aquarium.
   ___simple___
8. They talked and laughed on the way to the zoo.
   ___simple___
9. No, I don't like fried squid. ___simple___
10. The U.S. calls them astronauts, but the U.S.S.R. calls them cosmonauts. ___compound___
11. Either you apologize to your brother, or you stay in your room.
    ___compound___
12. Sandy told a ghost story, and Andrea made the popcorn.
    ___compound___
13. Fern is a wonderful gardener. ___simple___
14. Sue and Sally asked Rico and Ron to the big dance.
    ___simple___
15. Lorraine beats Bill at tennis, so she lets him win at checkers.
    ___compound___
16. I love to get up early and read the paper by myself.
    ___simple___
17. He walked to the edge of the cliff, and he looked down at the rocks. ___compound___
18. George Eliot's real name was Mary Ann Evans.
    ___simple___
19. Roberta saw a snake, and Albert caught a wild pig.
    ___compound___
20. Would you like to eat dinner or go to the park?
    ___simple___

PUNCTUATION

A. *Directions:* Insert the correct punctuation where it is needed in the following sentences. You may add *'s* when necessary.
EXAMPLE: Heres your hat Tom
         Here's your hat, Tom.

1. The two girls' books floated away.
2. Can't you find the house either, Myrtle?
3. "Yes, I'm doing my homework," Elsa said.

4. Don't touch that poisonous lizard!
5. Did you find Charles' coat?
6. Marie looked up and said, "I can't find the glue."
7. Ed couldn't go on the weekend trip, so Frank cancelled it.
8. Cheryl loves to eat shrimp, scallops, clams and lobster.
9. Wouldn't you like to see the Smiths' cat chase a mouse, Fred?
10. Oh, I'm afraid I'll have to skip the meeting tonight.
11. To cousin Will, Sam was a tremendous bore.
12. Get out of my flowers!
13. Dorothy told us that her mother's cold was better.
14. She said, "I'm going to bed," and went upstairs.
15. "Aren't you going to watch the girls' soccer team?" Kim asked.
16. Martha picked up her brother, brushed off his pants, and sent him home.
17. Ann isn't very friendly, but she's not mean.
18. In paragraph three above, your name is mentioned.
19. "Why can't you ever wear red, white, and blue clothes, Cornelius?" Amy inquired.
20. The sheep's farmer lives in that small hut, but he is rich.

B. *Directions:* Rewrite the following sentences using correct punctuation marks.

SMALL EXAMPLE: Slim likes fish!
           Slim likes fish.

1. Ann said "we should come to her house on Friday."
   Ann said we should come to her house on Friday.
2. "Are'nt you keeping score, Ed," I asked.
   "Aren't you keeping score, Ed?" I asked.
3. Judy likes beef chicken, and, pork, but she hates lamb.
   Judy likes beef, chicken, and pork, but she hates lamb.
4. Ouch. That shot really hurt doctor.
   Ouch! That shot really hurt, doctor.
5. Womens' clothes are more expensive than men's clothes.
   Women's clothes are more expensive than men's clothes.
6. "I should'nt have come to dinner" Edward said sadly?
   "I shouldn't have come to dinner," Edward said sadly.
7. Christine called her friend, and talked for three hours.
   Christine called her friend and talked for three hours.
8. Jane suddenly said "I've never read *Treasure Island*!
   Jane suddenly said, "I've never read Treasure Island."

9. Yes the Baxter's mouse died yesterday.
   Yes, the Baxters' mouse died yesterday.
10. "Robin Hood is a legendary hero," the teacher, said.
    "Robin Hood is a legendary hero," the teacher said.
11. Holly said that "she would'nt want her mother to see her grades."
    Holly said that she wouldn't want her mother to see her grades.
12. Against Uncle Red Sam didn't have a chance?
    Against Uncle Red, Sam didn't have a chance.
13. "Oh she doesn't know what shes talking about, Alice said coldly."
    "Oh, she doesn't know what she's talking about," Alice said coldly.
14. Tony saw Mary's house and he gasped at it's size.
    Tony saw Mary's house, and he gasped at its size.
15. "Her's is the best cider I've ever tasted." he said.
    "Hers is the best cider I've ever tasted," he said.

ERRORS

A. *Directions:* Each of the following sentences contains at least one error. Find each error and circle it.

SMALL EXAMPLE: Haven't we seen this movie before.

1. At the store there is many kinds of fruit.
2. I accidently sent the postcard to Tucson Arizona.
3. With her aunt Harriet went to the mountains.
4. John said that he would like to buy the new album.
5. Tazume gave his present to Alan, and Molly gave hers to Jeff.
6. "Oh, no" said Jared. "I didn't feed the dog."
7. We arrived in Florence Italy by train on Monday July 21, 1986.
8. The class read The Grapes of Wrath, a novel by John Steinbeck.
9. "Where are the coins" asked Hal.
10. Haven't you put the books on the shelves and the chalk in the drawer yet.
11. Joshua was worried that the package wouldn't arrive on time but Mrs. Henry said that its on its way.
12. Marc asked, 'When is sports classes meeting'.
13. Mary decided to recite Velvet Shoes by Elinor Wylie for the poetry contest.
14. Henry borrowed Janes notes because he had missed class on Tuesday.
15. "Shoot I missed the last bus," wailed Lou. "Now I'll have to walk two miles!"

16. Lydia packed her knapsack, canteen, sleeping bag, compass, and hiking boots for her hike in the Grand Canyon.
17. The group of firefighters and their spouses are traveling to Cleveland for a convention.
18. In the American West not only the cowboys but also the farmers chased away the buffalo.
19. Emma didn't attend the assembly, and her teacher, Ms. Irving, called Emma's home.
20. In the local newspaper, News of The Week, several meetings of the town council was announced.

B. *Directions:* Correct the error in each of the following sentences.

EXAMPLE: My mother gave her picture to my father, but Aunt Sue gave her's to me.   *hers*

1. Whenever you go   ...
2. Several of that type is found in the drawer.   *are*
3. The bicycle was just the one I wanted, but I didn't have enough money.
4. By Thursday Winifred still had'nt given Leroy the assignment for   *hadn't*
class.
5. We decided that the entire class will leave for Nova Scotia, Canada on Friday, August 17, 1993.
6. "Wow! I can't believe the leaves have already changed color!" exclaimed Jim. "Its only the beginning of September."   *It's*
7. Before you read any more of *Anne Of Green Gables*, take out the   *of*
trash, dry the dishes, and feed the cat.
8. Marion had to decide immediately whether to sign the letter "Yours truely" or Sincerely yours."   *truly*
9. After singing "Yankee Doodle," the children went outside, Benjamin fell down on the playground and had to be treated by the nurse.
10. There were tables of children's toys and clothing, men's and wom-ens clothing, antiques, and collectibles.   *women's*
11. I don't know whether I should leave immediately, or whether I should wait until the rain stops and perhaps be late?   *late.*
12. If you keep this dog, you must give away either your guppies or your boa constrictor.
13. "Where are the group of candidates for the election supposed to   *is*
meet?" asked Ned noisily.
14. The mysterious stranger arrived and whined irritably "Doesn't anyone remember my name?"   *No error*
15. Just because I gave you the biggest piece of cake   ...
16. Leaving the party early, Mr. and Ms Hughes went to Burger Bites   *Ms.*
and ate the Super Chewy Burger with home fries.

17. The post card arrived wrinkled and grimy, and I could barely make out the picture of lake Silver Bow with Mount Camel's Hump in the background.   *Lake*
18. Yesterday I went to school to take my history test and then I went to my piano lesson.   *,*
19. Not only does the Jefferson High school Student Council want to hold a dance, but it will do whatever is necessary to convince the school administration.   *School*
20. On Tuesday either you or I are going to run the movie projector, for Ms. Wang will be out of town at a teacher's convention.   *am*

2. King Arthur and Lancelot loved Guinevere.
   King Arthur loved Guinevere, and Lancelot loved Guinevere.
3. Demeter did not want to give up Persephone, and Hades, god of the Underworld, did not want to give her up either.
4. Greedy Midas loved gold, but he also loved his daughter.
   Greedy Midas loved both gold and his daughter.
   Greedy Midas loved gold and his daughter.
   Greedy Midas loved gold, and he loved his daughter.
5. Echo wanted to talk to Narcissus, but she could only repeat what he said.
   Echo wanted to talk to Narcissus and could only repeat what he said.
   Echo wanted to talk to Narcissus, and she could only repeat what he said.
6. Many people do not want to use either nuclear energy or solar energy.
   Many people do not want to use nuclear or solar energy.
   Many people do not want to use nuclear energy and do not want to use solar energy.
   Many people do not want to use nuclear energy, and they do not want to use solar energy.
7. Deborah or Peter would make a good president.
   Either Deborah would make a good president, or Peter would make a good president.
8. Zenobia must choose a pet, and she can choose either a cat or a dog.
   Zenobia must choose a pet, and she can choose a cat or a dog.
9. Helen of Troy was the most beautiful and the most faithless woman in the ancient world.
   Helen of Troy was the most beautiful woman in the ancient world, but she was also the most faithless.
   Helen of Troy was the most beautiful woman in the ancient world, and she was also the most faithless.
10. Sarah gave each person a card and gave each person a present.
    Sarah gave each person a card, and Sarah gave each person a present.

1. Will you walk the dog now, or will you walk him later?

2. James had not either cleaned his room or completed his homework.

James had not cleaned his room or completed his homework.

James had not cleaned his room, nor had he completed his homework.

4. On Tuesday Marion walked to school, and on Friday her father drove her.

6. Have the flowers or the balloons arrived yet?

7. Christopher Columbus set sail to find Asia, but he discovered America.

8. We will travel to Washington, D.C. and visit Williamsburg, too.

We will travel to Washington, D.C. and we will visit Williamsburg, too.

10. Neither Mortimer nor Janet had cleaned out his locker.

Mortimer hadn't cleaned out his locker, and Janet hadn't cleaned out hers.

Educators Publishing Service, Inc.
75 Moulton Street, Cambridge, Massachusetts 02138-1104

ISBN 0-8388-2238-X